Spirituality and Education

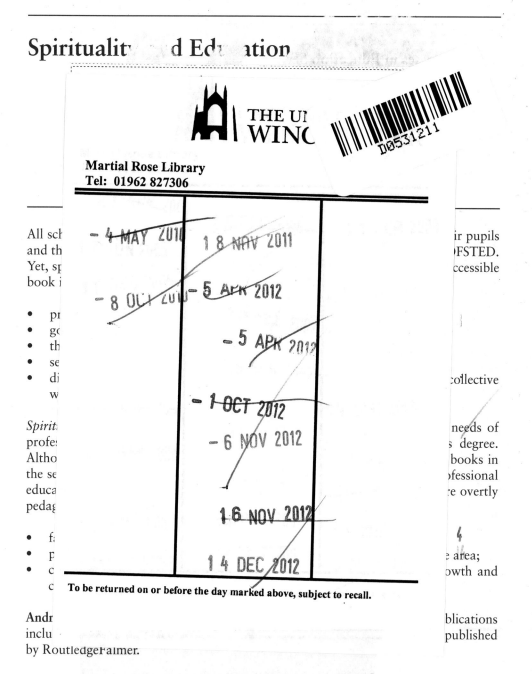

THE U[ ]
WIN[ ]

All sch[ ] ir pupils
and th[ ] OFSTED.
Yet, sp[ ] ccessible
book i[ ]

- p[ ]
- g[ ]
- th[ ]
- se[ ]
- di[ ] collective
  w[ ]

Spirit [ ] needs of
profe[ ] s degree.
Altho[ ] books in
the se[ ] ofessional
educa[ ] re overtly
pedag[ ]

- f[ ]
- p[ ] e area;
- c[ ] owth and
  c[ ]

Andr[ ] blications
inclu[ ] published
by Routledgeraimer.

Master Classes in Education Series
Series Editors: John Head, School of Education,
King's College, University of London and
Ruth Merttens, School of Education, University of
North London

Spirituality and
Education

Andrew Wright

London and New York

First published 2000
by RoutledgeFalmer
11 New Fetter Lane, London EC4P 4EE

Simultaneously published in the USA and Canada
by RoutledgeFalmer
29 West 35th Street, New York, NY 10001

RoutledgeFalmer is an imprint of the Taylor & Francis group

© 2000 Andrew Wright

Typeset in Sabon by Taylor & Francis Books Ltd
Printed and bound in Great Britain by TJ International Ltd,
Padstow, Cornwall

British Library Cataloguing in Publication Data
A catalogue record for this book is available from the British
Library

Library of Congress Cataloging in Publication Data
Wright, Andrew, 1958–
Spirituality and education / Andrew Wright.
    p.cm. – (Master classes in education series)
Includes bibliographical references (p.) and indexes.
1. Religious education – Great Britain. 2. Religion – Study and
teaching – Great Britain. 3. Spirituality. I. Title. II. Series.

LC410.G7 W77 2001
291.7'5–dc21   00–055223

ISBN 0–750–70909–X (hbk)
ISBN 0–750–70908–1 (pbk)

To Ruth, Bill, Richard and Lorna

Contents

Contents

Series Editors' Preface

It has become a feature of our times that an initial qualification is no longer seen to be adequate for lifelong work within a profession and programmes of professional development are needed. Nowhere is the need more clear than with respect to education, where changes in the national schooling and assessment system, combined with changes in the social and economic context, have transformed our professional lives.

The series, *Master Classes in Education*, is intended to address the needs of professional development, essentially at the level of taught masters degrees. Although aimed primarily at teachers and lecturers, it is envisaged that the books will appeal to a wider readership, including those involved in professional educational management, health promotion and youth work. For some, the texts will serve to update their knowledge. For others, they may facilitate career reorientation by introducing, in an accessible form, new areas of expertise or knowledge.

The books are overtly pedagogical, providing a clear track through the topic by means of which it is possible to gain a sound grasp of the whole field. Each book familiarises the reader with the vocabulary and the terms of discussion, and provides a concise overview of recent research and current debates in the area. While it is obviously not possible to deal with every aspect in depth, a professional who has read the book should be able to feel confident that they have covered the major areas of content, and discussed the different issues at stake. The books are also intended to convey a sense of the future direction of the subject and its points of growth or change.

In each subject area the reader is introduced to different perspectives and to a variety of readings of the subject under consideration. Some of the readings may conflict, others may be compatible but distant. Different perspectives may well give rise to different lexicons and different bibliographies, and the reader is always alerted to these differences. The variety of frameworks within which each topic can be construed is then a further source of reflective analysis.

The authors in this series have been carefully selected, Each person is an experienced professional, who has worked in that area of education as a practitioner and also addressed the subject as a researcher and theoretician. Drawing upon both pragmatic and the theoretical aspects of their experience, they are able to take a reflective view while preserving a sense of what occurs, and what is possible, at the level of practice.

Spirituality and Education

Although the 1988 Education Reform Act explicitly acknowledged the importance of spirituality within education, the realities which confronted the schools tended to deny scope for much work in this area. The creation of tests for the Key Stages in the child's school career and the publication of tables showing the test results for each school caused teachers and parents to focus attention on those aspects of schooling which were tested. Other work, in fields such as personal, social and health education, tended to be pushed to the margins of the school's activities. In this process concern about spirituality seemed to be of little relevance.

We can now witness a reaction against the constraints of this testing regime and a recognition that schooling has a wider remit. Part of this development has been a renewed interest in issues such as spiritual development. In some ways, this reaction echoes a wider concern within society. Although church going has continued to decline, there seems to be a change in the public *Zeitgeist*, a sense that we need something beyond instrumental knowledge to understand and ameliorate contemporary society.

Andrew Wright has therefore written a very timely book. It is difficult to write about spirituality as it is a most subtle and complex construct. In this clear and carefully constructed text we are steered through the arguments relating to all aspects of the topic. The quality of this narrative, combined with helpful overviews at the beginning and end of the book, bring clarity to this difficult but important subject. As such, we believe it makes a valuable addition to the literature of education.

John Head and Ruth Merttens
Series Editors

Acknowledgements

My thanks are due above all to John Head, who first floated the idea of this book and proved an invaluable source of advice and encouragement.

I also owe a debt of gratitude to my colleagues in the Centre for Theology, Religion and Culture at King's College: Ann-Marie Brandom, Mike Poole, Pete Ward and Andrew Walker.

A series of illuminating conversations with doctoral students at King's were invaluable in the early stages of preparation: particular thanks go to Jo Backus, Richard Cheetham, Janet Brannigan-Crogan, Alistair Falk, Fernando Gros, Neil Hopkin, Peter Manning, Viv Thomas and Tony Wenman.

Thanks are also due to those MA students at King's who read sections of the draft manuscript and offered invaluable comments: Chris Collingwood, Sue Cooke, Caroline Dunn, Natasha Fox, Martin Henwood, Ron Keating, Dom Mochan, Helen Paren and Wendy Worham.

Once again, I unashamedly plundered the professional and academic expertise of Angela Wright at the London Institute of Education.

The project would have been impossible without the love, patience and understanding of my wife Jacqueline and daughters Rebecca and Elizabeth.

Andrew Wright
Easter 2000

Introduction

Spiritual Images

What images does the word 'spirituality' conjure?

- Perhaps your first thoughts are Christian ones? Of sacramental worship on a Sunday morning in a rural parish church, the words, music and ceremony of the liturgy combining to evoking something of the 'beauty of holiness'? Of a gathering of evangelical Christians attentive to the message of the preacher expounding the Word of God? Of the silent contemplation of a Quaker meeting? Or of the charismatic exuberance of a Pentecostal congregation captivated by the refrains of a gospel choir?
- Or is your vision less parochial, extending beyond the boundaries of Christianity to embrace the stillness of the saffron-robed Buddhist monk lost in meditation? The rhythmic prayer of the tefillin-adorned Orthodox Jew? Or the wash of Muslim pilgrims circling the Ka'ba in Mecca?
- Or do your reflections simply bypass organised religion altogether, called to mind instead alternative spiritual traditions, such as the spirituality of the 'New Age' with its esoteric mixture of mysticism, gnosticism, astrology, reincarnation, aromatherapy, homeopathy, thought transference, flying saucers, and horoscopes?
- Or are your thoughts broader still, grappling with universal images of love and hate, life and death, war and peace, suffering and joy, futility and fulfilment?
- Or perhaps you find this whole exercise uncomfortable, as your ingrained suspicion of such crass piety reinforces your initial impression that this is probably not a book for you?

This exploration of the spiritual dimension of contemporary education aims to be as inclusive as possible: this is a book intended for religious believers and unbelievers alike, for those committed to a spiritual quest – whether it be religious or secular in nature – and for those cultured despisers disdainful of the entire pseudo-discourse of spirituality. The basic assumption is that spirituality and spiritual education are essentially controversial issues about which there is no public agreement. Consequently, I have written in the expectation of attracting a broad and frequently critical readership united only by a common concern for the integrity of spiritual education in our schools. Though I do not hesitate to offer my own particular slant on the present state of spiritual education, and to present a personal vision of its possible future development, my basic concern is not to encourage you to agree with me but rather to stimulate your critical thinking about the nature and place of spiritual pedagogy in contemporary education.

The Ambiguity of Spirituality

It is not so long ago that the philosophy of Logical Positivism – with its rejection of the language of spirituality as intellectually invalid, scientifically unverifiable and hence ultimately meaningless – was a dominant force in popular culture. The advent of a post-modern world, with its rejection of such pseudo-rationalistic dogma, has brought with it a revival of spirituality. For some, this renaissance is essentially religious, while others view it as the opportunity to celebrate the human spirit. Whatever its form, this spiritual revival is too diverse and deep-rooted to be mistakenly equated with the contemporary resurgence of religious fundamentalism. The majority of those committed to the recovery of a spiritual dimension in public and private life – believers and unbelievers alike – view with deep concern and suspicion 'that form of the return of the religious expressed in the often violent search for and affirmation of local, ethnic and tribal identities' (Vattimo, 1998, p. 80). At both popular and academic levels a reaction against the failures of modern rationalism, materialism and capitalism, coupled with a new-found freedom from the dogmas of traditional religious discourse, has helped create a renewed interest in spiritual questions, issues and values.

The world of education has not been immune to this spiritual renaissance. When the 1988 Education Reform Act introduced a system of schooling more concerned with attainment targets and performance tables than children's spiritual development, there seemed little prospect of spirituality constituting anything other than rhetorical icing on the educational cake. Few anticipated that, in a society in which the 'traditional cultures of spirituality ... are marginalised and silenced by the contemporary combination of bureaucracy, industry and the consciousness-creating media', spirituality would penetrate so quickly and so deeply into the fabric of our education system (Grimmitt, 1987, p. 120).

Spiritual education is with us, whether we like it or not, embodied in legislation and subject to OFSTED inspection. Consequently those of us involved in education have a professional responsibility to deal with the issue, regardless of the nature of our initial reactions, presumptions and prejudices, however favourable or unfavourable these might be.

The Aim of the Book

Spiritual Education is part of the *Master Classes in Education Series* and as such seeks to address the needs of professional development at the level of taught masters degrees. The book is aimed at teachers and lecturers, those involved in professional educational management, and all those with a professional interest in the cultivation of spiritual literacy in our schools. On the basis that spirituality constitutes a cross-curricular issue that carries implications for the life of the whole school I have assumed no prior specialist acquaintance with the question of spirituality and its place in the curriculum. Consequently specialist teachers of Religious Education will need to exercise a little patience in these areas in which I cover ground that will already be familiar to them.

The book is overtly pedagogical and as such aims to do the following:

- familiarise the reader with the vocabulary, language and landscape of contemporary spirituality;
- provide an overview of contemporary debate, research and curriculum development in the field of spiritual education;
- convey a vision of the possible future development of the subject by developing a set of positive proposals for a critical spiritual pedagogy concerned to cultivate the emergence of spiritual literacy.

The Task Ahead

The book is divided into three parts. Part I, The Landscape of Spirituality, explores the contours of contemporary spirituality, arguing that it is marked by significantly high levels of pluralism, diversification and ambiguity. After developing a provisional definition of spirituality (Chapter 1), contemporary spirituality is presented from the perspectives of the disciplines of philosophy (Chapter 2), theology and religious studies (Chapter 3), psychology (Chapter 4) and sociology (Chapter 5).

Part II, Contemporary Spiritual Education, begins with a historical review of the current renaissance of spiritual pedagogy (Chapter 6). Tensions within contemporary theory and practice are then discussed, with particular attention being given to the polarity between inclusive and exclusive approaches (Chapter 7). Finally, a liberal approach to spiritual pedagogy is explored and the suggestion made that it opens up the possibility of the emergence of a critical spiritual education (Chapter 8).

Part III, Towards a Critical Spiritual Education, begins by establishing some basic principles of critical spiritual education (Chapter 9), and goes on to set an agenda for its future development (Chapter 10). It is then suggested that the emergence of spiritual literacy is best served by a spiritual pedagogy that combines education as nurture (Chapter 11) with education as critique (Chapter 12).

Part I
The Landscape of Spirituality

1 What is Spirituality?

Part I explores the spiritual landscape of contemporary Britain through the perspectives of philosophy, theology, psychology and sociology. The present chapter lays the groundwork of this exploration by investigating the elusive nature of spirituality and establishing a working definition of spirituality as our *concern for the ultimate meaning and purpose of life*. The task of establishing appropriate levels of spiritual literacy, it is suggested, is particularly difficult in a pluralistic society in which there is no shared consensus about our ultimate beliefs and values. We are faced with a host of contrasting and conflicting spiritual options which continue to be the subject of fierce debate. It is unclear whether society is in the middle of a spiritual crisis or standing at the dawn of a new age of spiritual opportunity. One of the consequences of such uncertainty is that spiritual education will inevitably be a controversial issue in schools. This state of affairs does not, however, detract from the importance of the subject: it is precisely because spirituality is so problematic that there is an urgent need to develop pupil's spiritual knowledge, understanding and insight.

Towards an Understanding of Spirituality

Spirituality is a notoriously difficult term to define. Perhaps this ought not to surprise us, since at the heart of the spiritual is that which is inherently elusive and mysterious. Most of us will have encountered charismatic individuals who seem to have a unique depth to their being, a spiritual 'something' which we are able to recognise, but find almost impossible to pin down. Both the Hebrew and the Greek words for 'spirit', *ruah* and *pneuma* respectively, are rooted in the notion of the intangible movement of the air. According to John's Gospel, the Spirit of God, like the wind, 'blows where it pleases; you can hear its sound but you cannot tell where it comes from or where it is going' (John 3:8).

As well as being elusive and mysterious, the spiritual is also linked to that which is vital, effervescent, dynamic and life-giving. The person who is the 'life and soul of the party' will tend to animate those around them, breathing life and vigour into otherwise dreary proceedings. Towards the beginning of Hebrew scripture we read that 'God shaped man from the soil of the ground and blew the breath of life into his nostrils, and man became a living being' (Genesis 2:7).

At the heart of spirituality is that which is both mysterious and dynamic. As teachers we have all experienced the difference between a routine lesson and a lesson that 'comes to life' as the desire to grasp the elusive nature of the subject under investigation drives the class forward towards new levels of understanding.

Activity

- Get a large blank sheet of paper and brainstorm all the words and images that spring to mind when you reflect on the concepts 'spiritual' and 'spirituality'.
- Use different coloured pens to indicate connections and contrasts between the various ideas you have generated, and if possible try to cluster them into different groups.
- Now produce your own provisional working definition of spirituality in a sentence or short paragraph.

Among the definitions of spirituality offered by the *Concise Oxford Dictionary* are the following: (i) concerning the spirit as opposed to matter; (ii) concerned with sacred or religious things; and (iii) of a refined and sensitive soul.

Concerning the Spirit as Opposed to Matter

The distinction between mind and matter, which has its roots in the classical culture of ancient Greece and Rome, has had a significant influence on contemporary approaches to spirituality. Plato (*c*.428–*c*.348 BCE) viewed the material world as transient and contingent and contrasted it unfavourably with the spiritual realm of eternal and unchanging ideas. He believed that the idealistic domain of our mental processes was of a higher order than the empirical world of physical matter. This produces a dualistic anthropology which, by distinguishing between body and soul, encourages us to understand ourselves as 'ghosts in the machine', and 'spirits in the material world'. If we wish to establish an authentic spiritual life and take seriously questions concerning the ultimate meaning and purpose of existence, then it is imperative that we renounce the physical needs of our bodies and instead cultivate the well-being of our souls. If our bodies will ultimately revert to dust and ash, our immortal souls will live on, if not in paradise then at least in the memories of our loved ones. This belief that our inner spiritual nature is more important than the extent of our material wealth and possessions is reflected in contemporary attacks on the materialism and consumerism rife in Western capitalism, and in attempts to cultivate alternative non-materialistic life styles.

Concerned with Sacred or Religious Things

The material–spiritual dualism is rooted in the humanistic belief that our souls constitute the highest reality in the universe, and that the ultimate meaning of life is wrapped up with our spiritual well-being. However, many religious traditions hold that God – or some form of transcendent reality or power – stands at the centre of things, and that our spiritual lives should be driven by a quest for the sacred rather than the cultivation of our immortal souls. At the heart of this spiritual pilgrimage is a distinction between the sacred and the profane rather than between the spiritual and the material. To confuse the two by equating the sacred with the immaterial and the profane with physical matter can lead to a serious misrepresentation of some religious traditions. In the Western monotheistic traditions of Christianity, Islam and Judaism, for example, the material world is celebrated as a part of God's creation. Here the spiritual quest is conceived not as a means of escaping from the physical world but as a process of turning from all that is corrupt, sinful and displeasing to God in order to embrace all that is righteous, holy, and sacred. The rise of atheism has, for many, transformed the religious quest from a search for God to a search for ultimate meaning within an immanent and godless universe. Mircea Eliade notes how 'desacralization pervades the entire experience of the nonreligious man of modern societies and that, in consequence, he finds it increasingly difficult to rediscover the existential dimension of religious man' (1987, p. 13).

Of a Refined and Sensitive Soul

The third of our routes links authentic spirituality with the development of self-awareness through the exploration of our private inner-space and cultivation of our inner feelings and emotions. As St Augustine (354–430 CE) urged his readers: 'do not go outward, return within yourself ... in the inner man dwells truth' (Wright, 1996, p. 139). This particular understanding of spirituality illustrates the two routes we have already outlined: it is easy to equate our inner space with our immaterial souls, and link introspective reflection with those religious traditions which encouraged a contemplative life of private prayer and meditation. However, it is important to note that the cultivation of inner self-awareness does not require a dualistic distinction between mind and matter, and that religious devotion need not be limited to personal piety. The spiritual concern for self-awareness draws on the modern Western commitment to personal freedom and autonomy, a commitment which tends to produce an individualistic anthropology in which personal identity flows from introspective self-understanding rather than the quality of our relationships with others. Here our ultimate spiritual concern is rooted in self-acceptance, self-awareness and the establishment of a positive self-image, a concern that may be aided by contemporary 'self-help' techniques such as psychoanalysis and transcendental meditation.

If spirituality has to do with that aspect of the human condition which drives us forward in our quest to grasp the elusive mystery of the world, then these three routes establish a range of spiritual opportunities: spirituality may be conceived as a concern to emancipate ourselves from the constraints of the material world, as a search for the sacred, or as the exploration of our inner space.

Activity

- Compare your working definition of spirituality with the three perspectives outlined above.
- To what extent does your definition draw on the following:
    - (i) the contrast between mind and matter?
    - (ii) a distinction between the sacred and the profane?
    - (iii) the cultivation of self-awareness?

Spirituality and Ultimate Concern

The 1988 Education Reform Act stipulates that children are to be taught a balanced and broadly based curriculum which does the following:

- promotes the spiritual, moral, cultural, mental and physical development of pupils at the school and of society;
- prepares such pupils for the opportunities, responsibilities and experiences of adult life.

(HMSO, 1988, p. 1)

These broad educational aims can be read either (i) realistically, as presenting a down-to-earth concern to induct pupils into the moral norms of civilised society, or (ii) idealistically as – at a deeper and more profound level – concerned to open up the option of an education dealing with the ultimate spiritual destiny of humanity. This raises the question of the relationship between spiritual education and forms of moral, social, personal, cultural, civic and religious education.

There is a tendency to reduce headline-grabbing accounts of the alleged increase in levels of unruliness, violence and anarchy among young people to questions of 'mere' morality. The issue of the nature, quality and effectiveness of moral education is one frequently taken up by politicians, parents and social commentators. This debate frequently suffers from a tendency towards polarisation and politicisation, with the left-wing of British social opinion blaming the authoritarian instincts of the right-wing for the ills of society, the right-wing pointing a finger at the left-wing's preference for moral relativism, and both joining forces to present teachers as easily targeted scapegoats. But what is it that transforms a question about moral education into a question about spiritual education? What exactly is it that silences the moral rhetoric and forces us to address the fundamental *spiritual* questions?

It would seem that the shift from morality to spirituality occurs when humanity finds itself driven to the very edge of civilisation and forced to address the question of the ultimate meaning, purpose and nature of life. Often it is the sheer *horror* of events that impose such questions on us, as – for example – when on the morning of Wednesday, 13 March 1996 Thomas Hamilton entered the grounds of Dunblane Primary School in Scotland and proceeded to kill sixteen pupils and their teacher before turning a gun on himself. Responses to this, and to many other similar highly publicised incidents, can never be reduced to the level of 'mere' morality. It is not enough simply to label such events as 'bad' or 'illegal', and as we stumble towards the vocabulary of 'depravity', 'malevolence' and 'evil' so we are brought face to face with the question of the ultimate meaning and purpose of human existence. For many, the widespread violence, brutality, terror and inhumanity that characterise the twentieth century serve to undermine once and for all the possibility of spiritual complacency.

Activity

- Draw up a list of your own ultimate concerns.
- Interview professional colleagues about their understanding of the fundamental aims of education.
- Devise and carry out a classroom activity that will enable pupils to articulate and explore their understanding of the meaning and purpose of life.
- Keep a journal in which you record and comment on the core values expressed in the media, focusing especially on newspapers, television and advertising.

Transferring this argument to the classroom implies that ordinary education is transformed into spiritual education at that point when learning ceases to skim over the surface of a subject and instead begins to grapple with issues of ultimate meaning and truth that constitute the very marrow of our humanity. In Religious Education, for example, there comes a point at which mere 'learning about' religion metamorphoses into 'learning from' religion. Here religious teaching takes on a spiritual dimension, moving 'beyond an objective study of religions to an exploration of inwardness, a grappling with existential questions, a search for spiritual identity, an encounter with mystery and transcendence' (Slee, 1992, p. 42).

Routine education is transformed into spiritual education when pupils are brought to the threshold of ultimate meaning in the face of apparent absurdity. As Paul Tillich observes, 'such an experience presupposes that the spiritual life is taken seriously, that it is a matter of ultimate concern' (1962, p. 54). Without such ultimate concern, he argues, our lives lack passion, seriousness and creativity.

> The anxiety of meaninglessness is anxiety about the loss of an ultimate concern, of a meaning which gives meaning to all meanings. This anxiety is aroused by the loss of a spiritual centre, of an answer, however symbolic and indirect, to the question of the meaning of existence.
>
> (ibid., pp. 54f.)

On the basis of a distinction between 'preliminary' and 'ultimate' concern, Tillich identifies twin threats to an authentic spiritual life: an apathy that leads only to spiritual indifference, and a misplaced spiritual enthusiasm in which a preliminary concern is elevated to the status of ultimacy (1978, p. 13).

- *Spiritual apathy* – If we fail to make an appropriate distinction between preliminary and ultimate concerns then we run the danger of becoming indifferent to questions of fundamental importance and devoid of any genuine spiritual sense. As a result, we may find ourselves living as contented pigs rather than discontented philosophers, condemned like Sisyphus in Greek mythology to the futile task of repeatedly pushing a rock to the top of the hill, only to watch it continually roll back down again (Homer, 1946, p. 187).

- *Misplaced spiritual enthusiasm* – If, on the other hand, we raise a preliminary concern to the status of an ultimate one, the result is likely to be fanaticism or, in religious terms, idolatry. Such fanaticism can be comical, as in the archetypal anorak clad trainspotter, fashion victim or Internet surfer. However, it can also take on a more sinister dimension, for example among those whose ultimate concern is manifested in a bigoted affirmation of national, racial, or religious identity.

Spirituality, then, is rooted in a concern for ultimate meaning, purpose and truth, a concern that can be all too easily ignored or misdirected. Education becomes spiritual whenever a lesson – irrespective of the subject being taught – moves beyond a mundane level to grapple with issues surrounding the fundamental meaning and purpose of life.

The Spiritual Crisis of Modernity

In 1641 the French philosopher René Descartes (1596–1650) published his *Meditations on First Philosophy* (Descartes, 1969). It tells the story of his spiritual search for certainty and security in the midst of a chaotic world. 'Either there is some support for our being, a fixed foundation for our knowledge, or we cannot escape the forces of darkness that envelop us with madness, with intellectual and moral chaos' (Bernstein, 1983, p. 19). Descartes' solution to his dilemma was to turn inwards and trust nothing apart from his own immediate thoughts and experience. This basic idea is encapsulated in his frequently quoted formula '*Cogito ergo sum*' ('I think therefore I am'). Descartes' trust in the power of human reason became a cornerstone of the eighteenth-century Enlightenment, that cultural revolution that gave birth to the modern era and brought with it a wave of optimism about the future of humanity. Emancipation from the primitive superstition of medieval religion, coupled with dramatic advances in science and technology, suggested that we could now engineer our own salvation. This optimistic humanism later linked up with nineteenth-century evolutionary theory to create the modern myth of the inevitable intellectual, moral and spiritual progress of humanity.

This myth of progress was fatally undermined by events in the twentieth century: Auschwitz, Dresden and Hiroshima have become icons of a spiritual vacuum at the heart of western civilisation. Joseph Conrad, in his novel *Heart of Darkness*, first published in 1902, allows its chief protagonist, Kurtz, in an orgy of violence and insanity, to gaze into the depth of the human condition and in his dying words to articulate the sickness of the human spirit: 'The horror! The horror!' (Conrad, 1999). Francis Coppola's cinematic adaptation of Conrad's novel, *Apocalypse Now*, transfers Conrad's story from colonial Africa to the Vietnam War, thus allowing the terror Kurtz embodies to represent the full pathology of twentieth-century humanity.

For the philosopher David Levin, the polarisation between fact and value, objectivity and subjectivity, technology and spirituality, endemic in post-Enlightenment culture, has profound consequences for civilisation. Our subjective spiritual selves, he argues, have lost touch with reality and become self-destructive, no longer able to control the physical world explored by reason, described by science and manipulated by technology. 'When reason turned totally instrumental, a function solely of power, it legitimated the construction of a totalitarian state and engineered the Holocaust' (Levin, 1988, p. 4). After the Shoah, can anything ever again be genuinely pure or sacred?

There is no doubt that theology has struggled to come to terms with the depths of human depravity embodied in the Nazi concentration camps. Isabel Wollaston notes the variety of Jewish theological responses to the Holocaust: the turn to prayer and lamentation; the commemoration of the dead; the indictment of an absent God; the search for meaning and justice (Wallaston, 1992, p. 54). However, all too often the search for a theological answer fails, and the theologian is forced into silence. As Irving Greenberg notes with chilling simplicity: 'No statement, theological or otherwise, should be made that would not be credible in the presence of burning children' (Greenberg, 1977, p. 23).

The discourse of secular humanism fares no better than theology in its attempts to resolve the spiritual dilemma posed by the Holocaust. That the path of educated reason offers no easy solution is attested by one Holocaust survivor, Haim Ginott: 'My eyes saw what no [one] should witness: Gas chambers built by learned engineers, children poisoned by educated physicians, infants killed by trained nurses, women and babies shot and burned by High School and College graduates' (Ramsey, 1999, p,121).

As the French philosopher Michel Foucault comments: 'You may have killed God beneath the weight of all that you have said; but don't imagine that, with all that you are saying, you will make a man that will live longer than he' (1991, p. 211).

A basic question lies at the heart of the spiritual crisis facing contemporary society: 'What is the meaning, purpose and value of life in the light of the apparent failure of both religious and humanist discourse?'

Responses to the Spiritual Crisis

One response to the spiritual crisis of modernity has been to challenge the forces of secularisation that have marginalised Christianity and, it is claimed, produced a moral vacuum at the heart of Western civilisation. Nick Tate, Chief Executive of the Qualifications and Curriculum Authority (QCA), suggests that 'although many accept that truth in moral matters can be independent of God, the loss of the religious basis for morality has weakened its credibility' (Tate, 1996, para. 23; Beck, 1999, p. 153). He refers favourably to the Archbishop of Canterbury's argument that since the Enlightenment public morality has drawn on a residual belief in God, but is now unable to give an adequate account of the foundations of its received values. For some the solution is a simple one: if Britain's moral and spiritual decline is indeed the direct result of the eclipse of Christian belief, then this process must be reversed. Baroness Cox, for example, argues that education should aim 'to restore in our schools the centrality of Christianity as the major spiritual tradition of this land' (Bates, 1996, p. 96).

An alternative response has been to look to the future, to a post-modern spiritual affirmation that transcends the limitations of both religious and humanistic thought. For the American post-modern philosopher Richard Rorty the root of our spiritual malaise lies neither in the loss of a coherent religious vision of ultimate reality, nor in the eclipse of our capacity for spiritual experience in the face of modern rationalism (Rorty, 1989). Both of these solutions reflect attempts to impose absolute values on society and force us into a moral framework that limits our autonomy. For Rorty the only viable values are those we create for ourselves, and we must not allow our freedom of choice to be curtailed by the dogmas of either religion or humanism. Rorty seeks to maximise personal autonomy, the only limitation being the avoidance of cruelty, which he sees as a direct result of a failure to tolerate difference.

Activity

- List the pros and cons of Tate's Christian restorationism and Rorty's post-modern relativism.
- Which stance do you most identify with? Why?
- Which point of view is most clearly reflected in the general ethos of your school?
- Do you think that the tension between Tate and Rorty is inevitable? Are there ways of reformulating the problem?

These two snapshots of possible responses to the spiritual dilemma of modernity demonstrate the difficulties facing the spiritual educator. If there is broad agreement that society is in the middle of some form of spiritual crisis, there is no consensus surrounding either the nature of the crisis or possible solutions to it. For Tate the problem lies in the collapse of a shared moral framework, while for Rorty the dilemma is rooted in our failure to celebrate the diversity of world views. Is the problem that we are relativistic, or that we are not relativistic enough? Clearly any viable spiritual education will need to proceed by exploring this tension in greater depth.

Summary

- Spirituality is an elusive and dynamic concept whose complexity is revealed when viewed in the light of: a mind–matter dualism; the contrast between the sacred and the profane; and the notion of spirituality as the cultivation of self-awareness.
- Despite their differences, these three routes have in common a concern for the ultimate meaning, purpose and truth of human existence.

- The spiritual optimism of the eighteenth-century Enlightenment, fuelled by nineteenth-century evolutionary theory, gave way in the twentieth century to an age of anxiety which places a question mark over the viability of religious and humanistic affirmations of spiritual value.
- There is no consensus regarding possible responses to this spiritual crisis, as exemplified by the contrast between Tate's Christian restorationism and Rorty's post-modern relativism.

2 Philosophical Perspectives

How does spirituality, understood in the light of the previous chapter as concern for the ultimate meaning and purpose of life, manifest itself in British society? This chapter investigates a range of philosophical perspectives on contemporary spirituality. In doing so it rejects the stereotypical image of philosophy as a form of abstract speculation cut off from everyday experience, and instead suggests that the perspectives of materialism, romanticism, post-modernism and critical realism presented here play a formative role in the spiritual lives of children and young people. Succeeding chapters will explore the religious and secular dimensions of spirituality, unpack psychological research into spiritual experience and analyse sociological studies of prevailing spiritual attitudes and belief. The aims of this chapter are threefold:

- to illuminate the nature of spirituality in the light of a range of philosophical perspectives, on the assumption that a reciprocal relationship exists between philosophy and culture;
- to broaden the subject-knowledge base of spiritual educators, on the assumption that the better informed we are of our subject matter, the better our teaching is likely to be;
- to enable teachers to identify the philosophical roots of their own spiritual beliefs, on the assumption that it is impossible to sustain a philosophically neutral stance and that those who acknowledge their prior philosophical commitments are likely to be better educators than those who fail to do so.

The Legacy of the Enlightenment

The Enlightenment was an eighteenth-century cultural explosion that took Western Europe by storm, giving birth to a humanistic mind-set grounded in scientific reason and establishing the liberal principles of freedom and tolerance (Byrne, 1996; Outram, 1995). It was marked by important advances in learning in disciplines such as philosophy, science, medicine, politics, agriculture and history, and heralded revolutions in industrial production, technology, communications and transport. The Enlightenment marked the final break-up of the medieval synthesis of the classical culture of Greece and Rome and the monotheism of the Judaeo-Christian-Islamic traditions, a process which had begun years earlier during the Renaissance and Reformation. The chief legacy of the Enlightenment was a set of assumptions and principles that have come to form the basis of our contemporary modern culture, and which make up the mind-set of modernity. These include, among others, a commitment to the following:

- individual autonomy, responsibility and self-awareness;
- reason as the foundation of knowledge and understanding;
- a distinction between objective knowledge and subjective belief;
- the priority of science and technology over religion;
- the liberal values of freedom and tolerance;
- democratic politics.

Modernity has never been a monolithic culture. It consists of a diverse range of overlapping philosophical traditions and the interface between spirituality and philosophy is an extremely complex one, a situation that makes a comprehensive survey impossible in the present context. Instead, this chapter limits itself to a presentation of four major modern philosophical traditions that have been instrumental in shaping contemporary spirituality.

- *Materialism* – Initially the dominant tradition within modern culture was that of materialism which reduced reality to the sum of physical objects in the world and sought to *consolidate* the success of reason, science and technology.
- *Romanticism* – Reacting against the dominance of materialism, romanticism sought to *supplement* its commitment to reason by stressing the significance of the immaterial realm of human feeling and experience.
- *Post-modernism* – Both materialism and romanticism claimed to be able to arrive at relatively certain knowledge of the world, a position post-modernism sought to *transcend* by celebrating the contingency, relativism and inherent uncertainty of human understanding.
- *Critical realism* – Critical realism, responding to the challenge of post-modernity, sought to *reconstruct*, in a more subtle and sophisticated form, the modern commitment to human reason, and thereby rehabilitate the legacy of the Enlightenment.

Materialism

The roots of materialism lie in empiricism, the belief that knowledge is dependent upon sense experience. For John Locke (1632–1704) our ability to see, hear, touch, taste and smell produces ideas in our mind. We build up complex pictures of the material world by linking together these ideas. The simple ideas of 'round', 'green' and 'hard', for example, produce the complex idea of 'apple' (Locke, 1975). David Hume (1711–76) gave Locke's empiricism a sceptical turn, arguing that our empirical experience provides us with nothing more than a series of random sense impressions which we organise and structure in accordance with social convention (Hume, 1978). For Hume, empirical sensation offered 'a mere amalgam of piecemeal items of experience and impressions, with no underlying foundation on which knowledge of the self and the world could be established' (Byrne, 1996, 208f). In the early part of the twentieth century Logical Positivists sought to challenge Hume's scepticism by turning to the principle of verification. Any statement, they claimed, could – at least in principle – be tested against the empirical evidence and shown to be either true or false. They concluded that such scientific verification demonstrates that empirical experience can indeed provide us with secure and certain knowledge of the material world.

The success of empiricism in nurturing the growth of science and technology led to the increasing marginalisation of our moral, aesthetic and religious beliefs. Locke argued that, while our beliefs can never be held with the same certainty as scientific knowledge, they still have a vital role to play in the well-being of civilised society. Hume, however, insisted that our beliefs and values merely reflected social convention and subjective preference. The Logical Positivists went a step further, asserting that moral, aesthetic and religious truth claims are incapable of verification: we have no way of demonstrating empirically the rights and wrongs of euthanasia, the extent to which Beethoven's *Hammerklavier Sonata* constitutes great art, or whether or not God actually exists. Since such value statements were closed to the possibility of empirical verification, they could not be seen to be either true or false and instead were consigned to the status of – quite literally – meaningless emotivism. This led directly to a materialistic philosophy which claims that the physical world constitutes the sum total of reality, and that the realm of value can be reduced to the level of mere subjective preference.

It is beyond dispute that science and technology have made an enormous contribution to the material well-being of humanity. However, as we noted in the previous chapter, our abuse of technology can now no longer be ignored, and it is becoming increasingly clear that the growth of modern techno-science has not been accompanied by a parallel moral and spiritual renaissance. The result has been the dislocation of the realm of material fact from that of spiritual value. For Colin Gunton this 'divorce of the natural and the moral universes is perhaps the worst legacy of the Enlightenment, and the most urgent challenge facing modern humankind' (1985, p. 25).

Many philosophers believe that materialism gets itself caught up in an 'epistemic fallacy' which confuses our ability to know (epistemology) with the way things actually are in reality (ontology). Simply because scientific method offers more accessible and certain knowledge than moral discourse does not justify the conclusion that the realm of value is any less real, important or significant than the world of scientific fact. Reality, according to the critics of materialism, transcends our ability to comprehend it and consequently morality, aesthetics and religion cannot be dismissed as meaningless simply because they rely on informed judgements rather than scientific verification. Though materialism still has its defenders, many philosophers now adopt an increasingly sceptical attitude towards its dogmatic and cavalier dismissal of spiritual values.

> **Activity**
> - Draw up a list of the strengths and weaknesses of materialism and use it as the basis for developing your own considered response to a materialistic world view.
> - Use your journal to record examples of materialist attitudes in ordinary social encounters, in the media, in the staff room, around the school and in the classroom.
> - To what extent does materialism constitute a significant dimension of the spiritual values of contemporary society?

The decision to embrace such a materialistic philosophy has fundamental consequences for an understanding of spirituality, since our ultimate concerns and values cannot possibly be derived from any transcendent source or objective value system, but must instead follow from the assumption that there is no higher reality than the brute fact of the material world. Human freedom, for example, is frequently rejected in favour of forms of biological determinism, and the ultimate spiritual values of materialism tend to be limited to utilitarian notions of our physical well-being, comfort, security and happiness.

Romanticism

The romantic movement, which first flourished at the beginning of the nineteenth century and continues to play a key cultural role today, offers a significant challenge to materialistic philosophy (Wu, 1997). Romanticism affirms intuition and feeling as legitimate routes to knowledge and contrasts materialism's empirical philosophy with its own philosophical idealism. Where materialism follows a *convergent* model of truth, in which knowledge is dependent on the convergence of our minds with the physical world, romanticism adheres to a *coherence* model of truth, in which knowledge is dependent on the inner coherence of our ideas and experiences.

Where materialism points to the pragmatic success of techno-science, romanticism celebrates the cultural significance of literature, music and the creative arts. For the romantics a biological or chemical description of the human body can take our understanding of the human condition only so far, and must be supplemented by the depths of insight offered by creative artists. To dismiss the wisdom and insight of Shakespeare, Van Gogh and Mozart as ultimately meaningless is little more than philistine. That science appears on the surface to provide objective knowledge and the arts little more than subjective opinion is not a significant consideration, since our feelings and instincts reveal much more than reason can ever prove. Romanticism then seeks to rehabilitate the aesthetic, moral and religious discourse sidelined by materialism.

Romanticism owed much to Kant's belief that there we possess an innate mental ability to order and structure our experiences (Byrne, 1996, pp. 203–242). He held that we can never know the world as-it-is-in-itself, only the world as-it-appears-to-us, since our knowledge is always filtered through our unique perspectives and experiences. Our minds operate rather like a pair of spectacles: we cannot see without them, and what we can see with them is largely determined by the nature of the lenses. This means that, alongside procedures of scientific verification, we can legitimately appeal to our inner moral, aesthetic and religious sensibility as a way of discerning truth.

Hans-George Gadamer has argued that romanticism is essentially the mirror image of materialism. 'Belief in the perfectibility of reason suddenly changes into the perfection of the mythical consciousness,' resulting in the 'romantic reversal of the (rationalistic) criterion of the Enlightenment' (Gadamer, 1979, p. 243). In other words, when materialism affirms the significance of objective rational knowledge, romanticism counters by affirming the importance of subjective emotional intuition, or 'mythical consciousness'. As such, romanticism constitutes the flip-side of materialism: its strategy of identifying itself in terms of its opposition to materialism produces a 'romantic idealism where the human spirit [can] range at will, uncontrolled by scientific evidence or knowledge' (Torrance, 1980, p. 25).

The romantic affirmation of the authenticity of our unique personal and communal experiences has played a vital role in supporting liberal attempts to respond positively to the reality of cultural pluralism. Romanticism recognises the dangers of intellectual and cultural imperialism, in which those in positions of authority and power – frequently taken to be white, Western, middle-class, heterosexual, Christian males – impose their ideological beliefs and values on the disenfranchised and powerless.

One of the marks of the twentieth century has been the emancipation, of 'minority' groups from the domination of prevailing powers structures, primarily through the raising of levels of individual and group consciousness. Romanticism plays a significant role in helping to authenticate the cultural significance of 'difference' in human experience, understood in terms of sex, age, gender, ethnicity, sexual orientation, religious belief, socio-economic status, etc. It is to the twin liberal principles of tolerance and freedom that romanticism frequently turns as a means of binding the diverse cultural traditions that together constitute our pluralistic society. The freedom to hold fast to one's own particular experience of life brings with it the demand that one should tolerate the experiences of others.

The spiritual significance of romanticism in underpinning our pluralistic society is difficult to ignore. By resisting materialism romanticism seeks to: rehabilitate the discourse of morality, aesthetics and religion; free individuals to embark on their own spiritual quests; legitimate personal and communal experience; reinstate the spiritual question of life's ultimate meaning and purpose; and celebrate the reality of spiritual diversity.

Activity

- Draw up a list of the strengths and weaknesses of romanticism and use it as the basis for developing your own considered response to a materialistic world-view.
- Use your journal to record examples of romantic attitudes in ordinary social encounters, in the media, in the staff room, around the school and in the classroom.
- To what extent does romanticism constitute a significant diversion of the spiritual values of contemporary society?

Post-modernism

The philosophy of post-modernism has played a crucial role in late twentieth century culture (Woods, 1999). For the post-modern philosopher the greatest threat to our freedom comes from meta-narratives. For Jean-François Lyotard, who first introduced the term into philosophical debate, meta-narratives are comprehensive world-views which claim to explain the whole of reality (Lyotard, 1984). The world-views of religion, materialism and romanticism are all dependent on meta-narratives. In the post-modern world neither God, the material world, nor our immediate experience can provide final answers to the human condition. Such ultimate explanations of reality are not accessible to us, either due of our limited ability to understand, or simply because reality is itself inherently chaotic. The primary spiritual agenda of post-modernity is to enable us to do the following:

- deconstruct all meta-narratives that threaten to ensnare us in illusion;
- celebrate our freedom to roam through the post-modern cultural playground in which everything is permitted;
- continuously create and recreate our own personal spiritual fictions;
- imaginatively follow our personal preferences, inclinations and desires.

Post-modernism is not concerned to establish new truth, but to maximise our freedom through the deconstruction of the pseudo-truths encountered in meta-narratives, especially the prevailing ones of materialism and romanticism. These meta-narratives have their roots in the modern search for security which has elevated human consciousness to the centre of reality, whether in the form of rationalistic materialism or experiential romanticism. Foucault is adamant that we must 'abandon all those discourses that once led us to the sovereignty of consciousness' (1991, p. 202). Modernity, far from being the pinnacle of human achievement, is nothing but 'a momentary fold in the fabric of knowledge', a consequence of the need 'to think of man as the rational, autonomous dispenser of his own moral laws' (Norris, 1987,

p. 221). The picture of humanity constructed by the modern world is a fiction destined to be erased 'like a face drawn in sand at the edge of the sea' (Foucault, 1989, p. 387).

Jacques Derrida rejects (i) the theological assumption that words can encapsulate the revealed will of God; (ii) the materialistic assumption that language names objects in the physical world; and (iii) the romantic assumption that 'words are the symbols of mental experience' (Derrida, 1976, p. 11). When reading a text it is inappropriate to ask whether the words come from God, accurately picture reality, or properly represent the experience of their author. For Derrida, words cannot label either 'divine', 'physical' or 'mental' objects, instead they simply link up with other words in a never-ending web of language. Consequently we are free to surf the web of language without any need to search for an authoritative or canonical reading of the texts we encounter. We must learn to celebrate the freedom to read a text imaginatively and responsively, making use of it as we wish, according to our own desires and inclinations.

Activity

- Draw up a list of the strengths and weaknesses of post-modernism and use it as the basis for developing your own considered response to a materialistic world-view.
- Use your journal to record examples of post-modern attitudes in ordinary social encounters, in the media, in the staff room, around the school and in the classroom.
- To what extent does post-modernism constitute a significant dimension of the spiritual values of contemporary society?

According to Richard Rorty, such post-modern freedom demands that we hold fast to the liberal principles of freedom and tolerance if we are to avoid imposing our own assumptions on others. He defines liberals as 'people who think that cruelty is the worst thing in the world' (1989, p. xv). For Rorty it is our love of meta-narratives, with their authoritarian baggage and exclusive truth claims, that are a primary cause of cruelty in the world. The modern search for certainty and security has led us into the habit of imposing our beliefs and values on others. Such imperialistic attitudes must be countered by an ironic acceptance of our ignorance if we are to avoid cruelty. Rorty labels the person capable of living out such a vision a 'liberal ironist', one 'who faces up to the contingency of his or her own most central beliefs' and has 'abandoned the idea that these central beliefs and desires refer back to something beyond the reach of time and chance' (ibid.).

Post-modernity offers a highly original spiritual agenda, promising emancipation from religious and secular meta-narratives and the tyranny of a misplaced ultimate concern for absolute truth. Instead our only ultimate concern should be the ironic construction and reconstruction of our own spiritual identities in accordance with our own feelings, instincts and inclinations.

Critical Realism

Critical realism, which is fast emerging as a significant counter to what many see as the dogmatic excesses of post-modernity, sets out to avoid 'the alternatives of irrationalism and a positivistic conception of reality' (Collier, 1994, p. ix). It affirms an objective reality existing independently of our ability to experience it, a world which is 'structured, differentiated and changing' (Bhaskar, 1993, p. 4). This ontological reality is not something we are free to imaginatively create, but rather constitutes 'a unique truth ... waiting to be discovered, and providing a standard for the varieties of error' (Gellner, 1974, p. 48).

Critical realism has little time for post-modernity, which it takes to be fundamentally incoherent in putting forward the self-defeating 'truth claim' that all truth claims are illegitimate. In assuming that there are no ways of judging between alternative world-views, post-modernism actually legitimates all forms of belief, and so becomes a meta-narrative that 'licenses any and every form of dogmatism' (Collier, 1994, p. 14).

Romanticism, with its belief that we cannot pass beyond our particular experience of reality and encounter the world as it really is in itself, is similarly rejected by critical realism. It is not the case that our personal experience is always right, and it is possible to make informed and legitimate judgements between conflicting perceptions of reality. It is, according to critical realism, entirely appropriate to distinguish science from astrology, and to adjudicate between the relative literary merits of Jane Austen and Jeffrey Archer.

> Those who deny the right of a non-South African to criticise apartheid, or of the unanalysed to criticise psychoanalysis, or of men to criticise feminism, or of the unbelievers to criticise theology, are merely exposing their own bad intellectual conscience.
>
> (1994, p. 18)

Activity

- Draw up a list of the strengths and weaknesses of critical realism and use it as the basis for developing your own considered response to a materialistic world-view.
- Use your journal to record examples of critically realistic attitudes in ordinary social encounters, in the media, in the staff room, around the school and in the classroom.
- To what extent does critical realism constitute a significant dimension of the spiritual values of contemporary society?

The major problem with materialism is its tendency to simplify the world by reducing it to the sum of our empirical experiences. Roy Bhaskar, contrasting the surface realism of empiricism with the depth realism of critical realism, observes how scientific and humanistic exploration of reality has revealed deep underlying structures that are real even though not directly accessible to our sense experience. 'If we could ... taste the hydrogen and oxygen in water, we would not need to separate them by electrolysis' (1993, p. 31).

Stratified Reality

Physics, chemistry, biology, psychology, anthropology, sociology, literature, art, music and religion are but some of the diverse ways through which we are learning to understand reality. There is clearly a hierarchy at work here, since without the reality described by physics and chemistry there could be no reality explored by art, music and religion. However, the existence of such a hierarchy does not imply a reductionism in which higher levels are interpreted by lower levels: artistic creativity, for example, will be misunderstood if we try to reduce it to a form of biological behaviourism. As Michael Polanyi observes, 'it is as meaningless to represent life in terms of physics and chemistry as it would be to interpret a grandfather clock or a Shakespeare sonnet in terms of physics and chemistry' (1958, p. 382). Instead, the different levels of interpretation are best seen as complementary to one another.

Unity of Fact and Value

For Bhaskar the domain of value has as much ontological reality as the realm of fact. 'Nor do I think', he writes, that 'the objects of science exhaust reality. On the contrary, they afford only a particular angle or slant on reality, picked out precisely for its explanatory scope and power' (Bhaskar, 1993, p. 15). There is consequently a basic openness to the possibility of overcoming the modern distinction between fact and value and thereby recovering moral, aesthetic and religious realism. It is possible that the explorations of reality conducted by artists, scientists, philosophers and theologians will reveal that values are not mere human constructs, but are rather inherent in the very structure of reality.

Wisdom

Critical realism seeks to move beyond the modern polarisation of reason and feeling, logic and emotion, sense and sensibility. Polanyi describes a 'personal knowledge' in which reason, emotion and practical experience combine with our tacit physiological and mental awareness to produce an effective tool capable of exploring the complex structures of reality. Such wisdom is summed up in Bernard Lonergan's transcendent precepts: 'Be attentive. Be intelligent. Be reasonable. Be responsible' (Lonergan, 1973, p. 53).

Contingent Knowledge

Critical realism treads a path between absolute certainty and absolute relativism: we can obtain knowledge of reality, but such knowledge will always be contingent, always engaged in the process of striving for deeper understanding, always open to new insight. 'While there can be justified beliefs and there can be progress, there can be no final theory, unsusceptible to revision and improvement'(Collier, 1994, p. 23). As Polanyi puts it, with such a contingent rationality I can 'hold firmly to what I believe to be true, even though I know it might conceivably be false' (1958, p. 214).

The spiritual implications of critical realism are profound, since it suggests that we are not simply free to construct our own personal set of ultimate values, and instead must allow our spiritual identities to be shaped by our developing relationship with an objective reality which is inherently meaningful.

Activity

- Use the results of the four previous tasks set in this chapter to draw up an account of your own philosophical position, indicating the extent to which it draws on aspects of materialism, romanticism, post-modernism and critical realism.
- How does this philosophical position help shape and inform your understanding of the ultimate meaning and purpose of life?
- What light do materialism, romanticism, post-modernism and critical realism throw on the spiritual attitudes of society at large, of your professional colleagues, of your school as an institution and of the pupils in your care?

Summary

This chapter has identified four dominant philosophical trends within modern culture, each of which offers distinctive spiritual opportunities;

- Materialism proposes that our fundamental spiritual concerns must flow from the fact that ultimate reality is limited to the brute fact of our value-free physical universe.
- Romanticism suggests that our ultimate values will always be dependent on our own particular experience of reality.
- Post-modernism urges us to embrace the freedom to create and recreate our spiritual values at will.
- Critical realism suggests that the truth is out there, waiting to be discovered, and that our spiritual values need to conform to the values inherent in reality.

Spirituality and Religion

Any investigation of spiritual education cannot ignore the difficult question of religion. The issue is vexed since, in the context of an increasingly secular and pluralistic society, a high level of ambiguity surrounds the place of religion in society as a whole and within education in particular. After some preliminary remarks about the nature of religion and its place in schools this chapter identifies and unpacks five contrasting responses to the religious claim that our ultimate spiritual concerns should be directed towards God, or some form of transcendent reality. These are secular atheism, fundamentalism, traditional orthodoxy, religious liberalism and theological radicalism. Since the chapter assumes no prior formal engagement with the study of religion the Religious Education specialist may choose to skim through certain sections fairly quickly.

Religion and Education

A key feature of the modern trend towards secularisation has been the privatisation of religious belief. That is to say, in a religiously plural world individuals are held to be free to believe whatever they like, provided they don't allow their personal commitments to intrude excessively into the public sphere. Most of us will tolerate a staff room colleague with a strong religious faith, and may even have a sneaking admiration for them, but only if we can enjoy our break-time coffee safe from the fear that the conversation will constantly be manipulated around to religion. This norm of religious privatisation is clearly at odds with the fact that religion enjoys – through Collective Worship, Religious Education and cross-curricular spiritual education – a transparent and undeniably *public* place in the curriculum. The ensuing tension often produces resentment among teachers, leading to covert attempts to reinforce the unwritten rule of religious privatisation by deliberately side-stepping religious issues. However there are good reasons why teachers concerned with spiritual education need to bite the bullet and grapple seriously with the religious question.

- *Religion is a crucial dimension of spirituality* – Assume for a moment that the claims of Islam are true, that Allah did indeed created the world and reveal his will for humanity in the Qur'an. It follows that only Muslims, whose ultimate concern is rooted in submission to the will of Allah, can claim to possess a completely authentic spirituality. The ultimate concerns of non-Muslims, whether directed towards atheism, agnosticism or alternative religious beliefs, are simply mistaken. Similarly, the spiritual lives of all religious people are little more than illusion, effectively dislocated from the actual order of things, if atheists are correct in denying the existence of any form of transcendent reality. The point here is that the question of religious commitment is universal and unavoidable, and cannot simply be treated as an optional extra confined to religious believers. Atheism and agnosticism are just as much acts of faith as positive religious commitment, and whatever attitude we adopt towards religion – whether it be positive, negative or non-committal – will inevitably have fundamental implications for our spiritual lives and ultimate concerns. Because of this we cannot afford to bracket out religious issues when attending to spiritual education.

- *Religion is an inevitable dimension of schooling* – It is impossible to ignore the fact that religion in general, and Christianity in particular, continues to play a significant role in schools: our education system is founded on a partnership between the state and the established Church of England; an increasing number of schools have religious foundations; Religious Education is a compulsory subject; and the law makes it clear that Collective Worship cannot be reduced to a mere assembly of pupils and staff for pastoral or administrative purposes, but must – under normal circumstances at least – be a distinctively religious activity. Whether we like it or not, religion is ingrained in our education system, and consequently it is imperative that teachers develop an appropriate professional response to the issues it throws up.

- *Religion is a controversial issue within the school community* – In my experience, most teachers occupy the middle ground between the extremes of zealous belief and militant atheism. Many of these also accept that religion is an issue that needs addressing, but feel that they lack the necessary knowledge, skills and insight to do so successfully. The instinct to 'leave well alone' often creates a vacuum exploited by those at the extremes of the religious–secular divide with an axe to grind. The result can be the injection of a combination of resentment and confusion into the very core of the spiritual life of a school. The only appropriate educational response to the fact that religion is a controversial issue within the school community has to be that of a professional and educative engagement with the issues, since turning a blind eye will merely serve to exacerbate an unhealthy situation.

Activity

- Note down your own attitude towards religion.
- Would you describe yourself as an atheist, an agnostic or a believer? Why?
- Do you agree with the case outlined above that religion should have a public place in schools precisely because it is a controversial issue?

Bracketing out the religious dimension of spirituality is, then, not a viable educational option. Consequently it is important that we develop an understanding of the various spiritual options that flow from religious belief. Our concern is not directly with the phenomena of religion, and there is no attempt to outline the basic beliefs and practices of the world's religious traditions. Instead, taking a lead from our understanding of spirituality as *ultimate concern*, the focus will be on identifying a variety of truth claims concerning the nature of *ultimate reality* that emanate from religion. The presentation that follows outlines five basic reactions to the claims to ultimate truth made by the world's religions. It does not claim to be exhaustive, but simply offers a representative sample of responses to the issue of religious truth in contemporary society.

Secular Atheism

For many believers knowledge of God is the result of a divine revelation embodied in historical events, inscribed in sacred scripture, manifested in spiritual experience and authoritatively transmitted by a faith community. The Enlightenment directed a hermeneutic of suspicion towards all such traditional sources of religious authority, and insisted instead on reason as the only proper path to knowledge (Buckley, 1987; Kung, 1980). This led to the decline of traditional revealed theology rooted in notions of divine revelation, in favour of a natural theology grounded in human reason. Such natural theology set out to demonstrate a rational justification for belief in God. Revealed theology 'from above', rooted in God's search for humanity, was replaced by natural theology 'from below', rooted in the human search for God.

There is today a general consensus that the various rationalistic 'proofs' of God's existence fail to provide an adequate intellectual foundation for religious belief. Just as significantly, many religious believers find them to be spiritually inadequate: a God who does no more than create a mechanical universe and then leaves it to its own devices is not a God worthy of worship. As the philosopher and theologian Blaise Pascal (1623–62) pointed out, the deistic 'god of the philosophers' lacks the personal and redemptive attributes of the 'God of Abraham, Isaac and Jacob' (Pascal, 1966).

With both philosophers and theologians unhappy with the God offered by Enlightenment reason the implausibility of religion became increasingly evident, at least in some intellectual circles. This led to a revised agenda, in which the task was no longer to demonstrate the existence of God but to explain the persistence of religion despite its lack of any rational foundation. The lead here was given by Ludwig Feuerbach (1804–72). Reversing the Judaeo-Christian formula that 'God created human beings in his own image', he suggested instead that it was 'human beings who created God in their own image' (Feuerbach, 1989). By accounting for the human need to project the idea of a god with human features one would also explain the continuing attraction of such an intellectually implausible hypothesis. Such accounts were provided by, among others, Karl Marx (1818–83), Friedrich Nietzsche (1844–1900) and Sigmund Freud (1856–1939):

- *Freud* viewed the idea of God as a neurotic projection, arguing that we have a psychological need to create an ideal father figure once we recognise the fallibility of our actual fathers.
- *Marx* saw religion is the 'opium of the people', a means of social repression whose function is to protect privilege in an unequal society by encouraging the poor to accept their lot in the light of the promise of future recompense for their sufferings in heaven.
- *Nietzsche* claimed that religion serves to offer us a false security which, by dumbing down the human spirit, produces contented pigs instead of discontented philosophers and limits access to a life-affirming 'will to power'.

Dubbed by Paul Ricouer the 'masters of suspicion', this triumvirate helped bring into being a modern mind-set hostile to religion and lacking in religious sensibility. As David Hay puts it:

> the European experience over the past few centuries has led to a profound suspicion, not to say contempt, or in some cases hatred, of the religious institution, in large sectors of society ... it is this hermeneutic that people engage in when they conceive of their experience of the sacred as illusion, as the lies of consciousness.
> (1985, pp. 140ff.)

There is no agreement about the spiritual implications of this loss of religious sensibility. For some, the 'Enlightenment affirmation of "self without God" in the end negated itself because reason, as means, was left, in the absence of God's truth, without any spiritual or moral goal' (Harvey, 1990, p. 41). A position challenged by Marx and Engels in the *Communist Manifesto*: 'All that is solid melts into air, all that is holy is profane, and men at last are forced to face with sober sense the real conditions of their lives and their relations with their fellow men' (ibid., p. 100). We are clearly in complex and controversial territory. Among the consequences of atheism we may list the following:

- a shift in focus from transcendence to immanence, seeking spiritual fulfilment 'here below' rather than 'up above';
- a relocation of the source of ultimate spiritual value from God to the personal, social and material;
- the creation, discovery or affirmation of a set of ultimate human goals in the midst of a godless universe;
- the emergence of utilitarian and pragmatic forms of moral discourse;
- the rise of hedonism, materialism and consumerism;
- the establishment of life affirming and spiritually astute forms of atheistic humanism.

Forms of Fundamentalism

It is a reflection of the religious illiteracy prevalent in some sections of society that any group that holds fast to a distinctive religious belief quickly finds itself labelled 'fundamentalist'. The use of a single abusive term reveals a lack of subtlety and insight in responding to the multi-layered issue of religion. Such a loose use of language ignores the complexity of religion and runs roughshod over the liberal principles of open-mindedness, charity and tolerance. In particular, it ignores the fact that in many religious traditions the emergence of fundamentalism represents a distinctively modern aberration from orthodox belief and practise.

Fundamentalism cannot simply be equated with (i) social and political militancy, unless one chooses to define Mahatma Gandhi or Martin Luther King as fundamentalist; (ii) a refusal to conform to the rational norms of modern post-Enlightenment society, unless one adopts an imperialistic attitude towards non-occidental rationality and reject *a priori* all religious traditions as irrational superstition.

Roy Bhaskar has argued that the problem of fundamentalism is that it seeks to start from scratch (1993, p. 76). Fundamentalism tends to combine a positivist epistemology in which the believer has direct and unmediated knowledge of God with a hermeneutical naïveté in which God's will is assumed to be transparent, non-negotiable and not open to interpretation.

On this basis it is inappropriate, for example, to label all Evangelical Christians as 'fundamentalist' simply because they believe that 'the Bible and its doctrine should be the absolute controlling authority, under God and under Jesus Christ, of the doctrine of the church and the practice of Christians' (Barr, 1980, p. 65). Mainstream Evangelical scholarship accepts that the revelation contained in the Bible, though divine, is mediated by the same historical processes as any other literary document, and that authentic biblical interpretation requires a hermeneutic depth that does not simply skim the surface meaning of the text. Thus, for example, St Paul's statement 'Slaves, obey in everything those who are your earthly masters' (Colossians 3:22) needs to by read in the light of his claim that 'In Jesus Christ you are all sons of God ... there is neither slave nor free' (Galatians 3:26ff.), as well as in the light of the cultural norms of the first-century classical world, if an Evangelical Christian is truly to discern the will of God in such matters. This has little to do with a fundamentalism that asserts 'that the doctrinal and practical authority of scripture is necessarily tied to its infallibility and in particular its historical inerrancy' (Barr, 1980, p. 65).

If we accept this identification of fundamentalism with absolute and non-negotiable knowledge, then we are forced to acknowledge a range of fundamentalist traits within secular culture. There are many non-religious forms of political, cultural and social fundamentalism which, embracing positivist ways of knowing and retaining hermeneutical naïveté, remain closed to the 'other' and are consequently severely limited in their ability to grasp an adequate sense of life's ultimate meaning and purpose.

Fundamentalism, properly understood, has more to do with the absolutist manner in which ultimate beliefs are held and acted upon rather than their material content. Both religious and secular forms of fundamentalism ought to be treated in the classroom as pathological and counter-educative. This suggests that the use of the term 'fundamentalism' within spiritual education ought not to be used not as a means of bracketing-out religious questions, but as a means of enabling and encouraging pupils to critically discern and challenge the pathological traits within both religious and secular traditions.

Activity

Most people in Britain use a single word to label the phenomenon of 'snow', while the Inuit require a much richer and more extensive vocabulary if they are to survive and flourish in sub-zero conditions.

- Brainstorm the range of vocabulary currently available to you as you set about the task of analysing and evaluating religious belief.
- Do you agree with the suggestion that religiously illiteracy is widespread in contemporary society, and that this is – at least in part – due to a lack of appropriate language?

Traditional Religious Orthodoxy

The fact that the plausibility structures of contemporary society tend to be antithetical towards religion does not justify the simplistic equation of religion with fundamentalism. Instead, a contrast needs to be drawn between religious orthodoxy and religious fundamentalism. The term 'orthodoxy' is being used here to refer to mainstream forms of religious belief, operating within (relatively) clearly identifiable historical traditions such as Buddhism, Christianity, Hinduism, Islam, Judaism and Sikhism. The use of the term is not intended to be restricted to notions of 'true doctrine' and 'right belief', but instead to encapsulate the entire experiential world-view of a religious tradition as it is both thought-out and lived-out.

An orthodox religious tradition will generally seek to consolidate its identity by drawing on its inner resources, internal coherence and received wisdom, rather than through a fundamentalist reaction to the threat of secular culture. Orthodoxy does not normally follow the route of a fideistic withdrawal from modern society in favour of a 'surrogate such as God, social convention or custom which cannot be rationally justified' (Bhaskar, 1993, p. 398). Instead it is likely to prefer the option of a critical engagement with the plausibility structures of contemporary society in order to dispute the moral, intellectual and spiritual high ground.

An illuminating example of this apologetic process of engagement-and-challenge is to be found in the expansion of early Christianity. It has been argued, with a certain degree of plausibility, that the first Christian theologians 'developed a view of the world and of human society which formed a victorious alternative to classicism', and consequently the early Church flourished 'because in certain respects it proved itself intellectually superior to a bankrupt alternative' (Gunton, 1983, p. 1).

Students of religion increasingly recognise the importance of colonial discourse analysis, which explores ways in which 'representation and knowledge are expressions of material and political power' (Flood, 1999, p. 231). Such analysis throws light on the phenomenon of 'Orientalism', the colonisation and misrepresentation of non-Western religious traditions by modern occidental modes of thought, in which 'the Orient becomes a projection of what the West does not wish to acknowledge about itself' (ibid.; cf. also Said, 1978). While the charge of Orientalism is generally applied specifically to European colonialism and imperialism, a process closely linked with Christian missionary activity, it is becoming increasingly clear that in general terms Western academic discourse continues to distort and marginalise traditional forms of orthodox religious belief. A school that elects to bracket out religious questions is, in effect, imposing a post-Enlightenment world-view on orthodox religious traditions.

The picture of a diversity of orthodox religious traditions holding fast to their pre-modern world-views and engaging critically with the prevailing plausibility structures of modernity is not one commonly recognised by those mesmerised by secular presuppositions. Nevertheless it is, I suggest, an important dimension of contemporary culture. The fact that the vast majority of religious believers hold fast to a set of ultimate beliefs and values that point beyond this world to some form of transcendent realm, and attempt to do so without recourse to fundamentalism, is a significant factor in the panorama of spiritual options available to humanity today.

The task here has not been to (i) predict who the likely winners might be in this continuing debate; (ii) defend religious orthodoxy; or (iii) describe the rich variety of spiritual beliefs and values associated with orthodox religious traditions; but rather (iv) to present the case that any viable spiritual education must take adequate account of those (in the main) pre-modern religious traditions which claim an intellectual, spiritual and moral integrity greater than that possessed by our prevailing Western culture. Failure to do so will lead only to a liberal imperialism that undermines its own cherished principles of tolerance and charity.

Religious Liberalism

For the Protestant theologian and founder of modern theology, Friedrich Schleiermacher (1768–1834), the conflict between religion and secular culture was neither necessary nor inevitable. Rejecting the options of (i) living in a fundamentalist ghetto; (ii) adopting an orthodox stance in tension with the norms of modernity, or (iii) jettisoning his Christian faith, he sought an alternative way forward: (iv) a theological liberalism capable of reconciling religion with the modern world.

Schleiermacher begins his project by rejecting both a traditional religious reliance on *revelation*, and the modern trust in *reason* as sources of theological knowledge. Instead he turned to the emergent tradition of romanticism which, as we have already seen, identified *inner feeling* as a legitimate way of understanding the world. The foundation of religious belief, he claimed, is neither revelation nor reason, but the religious sense of 'being absolutely dependent ... of being in relation with God' (Schleiermacher, 1976, p. 12). Religious doctrine constitutes the outer expression of such inner religious sensibility: 'Christian doctrines are accounts of the Christian religious affections set forth in speech' (ibid., p. 76).

This enabled Schleiermacher to replace a traditional *cognitive-prepositional* model of religion in which religion is rooted in dogmatic truth claims, with an *experiential-expressive* model in which religion is rooted in our capacity for transcendent experience (Lindbeck, 1984). As a result Schleiermacher claimed that religious dogma, rather than being dismissed as no more than a superstitious and pseudo-scientific attempt to describe the world, ought to be embraced as a profound expression of our inner religious sensibility. By follow the romantic strategy of embracing inner experience as a route to knowledge Schleiermacher sought to enable religion to take its rightful place as a legitimate and indispensable dimension of modern culture, enhancing rather than contradicting scientific discourse.

A further challenge facing those religious believers who wished to reconcile their faith with modern culture was the need to account for the conflicting truth claims made by the various religious traditions. On the basis of a cognitive-prepositional model of religion, in which doctrine makes objective claims about the nature of reality, the acceptance of the truth of one religious tradition normally brings with it the denial of the truth of all the others. For example, if Jesus of Nazareth is indeed God incarnate, as Christians claim, then he is neither the prophet of God proclaimed by Islam, nor the false prophet rejected by Judaism. This presents problems for those who wish to live in a liberal world governed by the principles of freedom and toler-ance, since to hold fast to the exclusive truth of one religious tradition entails rejection of all others, and quickly draws the accusation of moral intolerance and intellectual arrogance.

Adopting an experiential-expressive model of religion offers the believer a way out of this dilemma. Observing the remarkable similarities between the prayers of most religious traditions, despite their conflicting truth claims, John Hick argues that:

> Such prayers and hymns as these must express, surely, *diverse encounters with the same divine reality*. These encounters have taken place within different human cultures by people of different ways of thought and feeling, with different histories and different frameworks of philosophical thought, and have developed into different systems of theology embodied in different religious structures and organisations. These resulting large-scale religio-cultural phenomena are what we call the religions of the world. But *must there not lie behind them the same infinite divine reality*?
>
> (Hick, 1977, p. 143, my italics)

For Hick there is no real conflict between the world's religious traditions, since they are made up of secondary and culturally diverse expressions of a primary and universal religious experience. As a result, the narrow exclusivist truth claims of particular religious traditions may give way to a universal religious sensibility that cuts across cultural, national and ethnic divides.

This possibility of a universal spirituality, drawing on the insights of all religious traditions, has become a significant option in contemporary culture. Those religious believers who accept a liberal experiential-expressive theology are able to affirm the following:

- ultimate spiritual concerns that are specifically religious and do not require disengagement from the mainstream of modern culture;

- access to knowledge of transcendent reality rooted in the capacity for inner-experience and spiritual sensibility;
- freedom to adopt an inclusive universal theology that side-steps the need to select between a range of exclusive parochial alternatives.

Radical Non-Realistic Theology

We must glance briefly at one final spiritual option that forms part of the religious quest. Atheism, fundamentalism, orthodoxy and religious liberalism constitute contrasting meta-narratives: each offers a complete account of the actual nature of reality and embodies a distinctive and exclusive truth claim. This includes the universalism of religious liberalism which, despite the surface appearance of being open to a diverse range of religious beliefs, actually affirms the distinctive and exclusive truth claim that all religious traditions represent equally valid vehicles through which a common experience of a transcendent reality may be obtained. Acceptance of any of the four positions outlined above requires the rejection of the other three. It is immediately obvious, in the light of the discussion in the previous chapter, that such meta-narratives run against the grain of post-modernism. As we have seen, the post-modern world-view is concerned to deconstruct all such meta-narratives. Theological engagement with this post-modern agenda has resulted in forms of radical theology.

Perhaps the most prominent of the radical post-modern theologians working today is Don Cupitt, who remains an Anglican priest despite his advocacy of a thorough-going non-realist theology which denies the actual reality of God. In his classic book *Taking Leave of God* he rejects the moral and intellectual possibility of belief in an objective God, yet insists that 'it is vitally important to try to preserve something of the spirit of religion even though its institutional and doctrinal aspects appear to be in irreversible decay' (Cupitt, 1980, p. 2). Cupitt goes on to advocate a radical spiritual autonomy grounded in the belief that 'people increasingly want to live their own lives, to make their own choices and to determine their own destinies' (ibid., p. 3). Our religious language, he claims, can only skate over the surface of reality, and consequently we are free to continually construct, deconstruct and reformulate a range of ultimate spiritual concerns on the basis of our private desires, preferences and inclinations (Cupitt, 1987). What distinguishes Cupitt from secular post-modernists is his belief that the language and artefacts of traditional religious culture can be useful tools and objects in the game of DIY spirituality.

Summary

- The chapter began by suggesting that the controversial nature of religion needs to be confronted in schools rather than swept under the carpet.
- The various spiritual options that flow from the acceptance, reformulation or rejection of religion were then explored in terms of a range of conflicting ultimate truth claims.
- Atheism, traditional religious orthodoxy, liberal religious universalism and radical theological non-realism constitute a complex range of spiritual possibilities.

- If we fail to engage with any of these possibilities in an informed, reflective, educative and spiritually sensitive manner we run the risk of slipping into closed and pathological forms of fundamentalism.

Activity

- How are your religious attitudes – whether positive, negative or non-committal – reflected in your current approach to spiritual education in the classroom?
- Describe the prevailing religious attitudes of your professional colleagues and pupils in your school. To what extent do they reflect the following:

  (i) atheism;
  (ii) traditional religious orthodoxy;
  (iii) liberal forms of religious universalism;
  (iv) types of radical anti-realistic theology?

- Can you identify any issues surrounding the religious dimension of spirituality that this chapter has failed to address?

---

4   The Psychology of Spiritual Experience

Against the background of a preliminary definition of spirituality as 'ultimate concern' the previous two chapters have shown how philosophical and theological considerations throw up a diverse range of spiritual possibilities. The task of the present chapter is to add a psychological dimension to the emerging landscape of contemporary spirituality by exploring empirical research into the extent and nature of spiritual experience with particular reference to children's spirituality.

Spiritual Experience and Empirical Research

The current government guidelines on spiritual education present spirituality in terms of a sense of awe and wonder in the face of the mystery of existence. Jack Priestley represents such mainstream educational thinking when he notes that 'spiritual awareness manifests itself first of all in feelings and emotions from which it has to be translated into thought if it is to be talked about at all' (1985, p. 114). Alongside this commitment to the importance of spiritual sensibility is a tendency to present spiritual experience as a far broader phenomenon than religious experience. Spiritual education has accepted 'the necessity to turn to a more holistic model of human spirituality, which sees it as something larger than any individual religion' (Hay and Nye, 1998, p. 53). There can be little doubt that the psychological interest in spiritual experience carries far greater weight than philosophical and religious reflection in giving a lead to current educational policy and practice.

Empirical research into children's spiritual experience is a relatively recent addition to a long standing tradition of scientific exploration of adult religious experience. Exploration of the spirituality of children and young people has flourished in the last twenty-five years, and the body of research literature is expanding rapidly, both in terms of its quantity and its quality. The present task is to review this research and identify some of its key conclusions. In the space available it is necessary to be highly selective, and more comprehensive surveys are readily available for those who wish to explore the issues raised in greater detail. The chapter begins by sketching in the background to the research before offering a brief survey of key investigations into children's spirituality since the mid-1960s. Attention then turns to two major research projects which have had a significant impact on spiritual pedagogy in recent years: the Children's Spirituality Project, based at the

University of Nottingham under the direction of David Hay, and the Children and Worldviews Project, based at the Chichester Institute of Higher Education under the leadership of Clive Erricker.

Religion as Manifestation and Proclamation

The key to understanding the theoretical basis of the research tradition concerned with the spiritual lives of children lies in Descartes' identification of the two basic substances that he held constitute reality: mind and matter. This dualism made possible two distinctive ways of interpreting religious language: as a cognitive description of objective reality, or as an affective expression of subjective experience. Paul Ricoeur, in exploring the tension between these two approaches, identifies two conflicting hermeneutical procedures, which he labels respectively 'phenomenology of manifestation' and 'hermeneutic of proclamation' (Ricoeur, 1995).

He offers as an example of the 'phenomenology of manifestation' the work of Mircea Eliade (1987). According to Eliade, religion is best understood as an encounter with the numinous or holy, which manifests or reveals itself through a 'hierophany' or sacred experience. A hierophany takes the form of a primary pre-linguistic experience of the natural world, which is then given a secondary articulation in sign, symbol, language, ritual and artefact. This is clearly a version of the experiential–expressive model of religion encountered in the previous chapter.

As an example of the 'hermeneutic of proclamation' Ricoeur proposes the self-understanding of the Judaeo-Christian tradition. 'With the Hebraic faith,' he argues, 'the word outweighs the numinous ... the numinous is just the underlying canvas from which the word detaches itself' (Ricoeur, 1995, p. 56). In the story of Moses and the Burning Bush, for example, the experience of holiness Moses is confronted with is entirely secondary to the Divine Word proclaimed by God (Exodus 3:1–4:17). The theological burden of the narrative is carried by God's instructions to Moses, rather than by Moses' religious experience and the description of the theophany is completed within the first six verses of the extended narrative. Consequently the Hebraic tradition is generally suspicious of the natural world as a source of revelation, normally equating images and symbols drawn from religious experience stimulated by the natural world with idolatry.

This distinction between manifestation and proclamation, and in particular the widespread preference for manifested experience over against linguistic proclamation, is crucial for understanding assumptions made within the research tradition under review here regarding (i) the nature of religion; (ii) the foundations of empirical research into the psychology of spiritual experience; and (iii) educational conclusions drawn from such research.

The Nature of Religion

Ever since Schleiermacher first articulated the experiential–expressive model of religion academic study of religion has tended towards a preference for a theology of manifestation. Thus, for example, we find in the early anthropological investigation of primal religion conducted by Robert Marett (1866–1943) 'mana' being identified as an occult force manifested through a range of objects, individuals and rituals. 'Savage religion … is something not so much thought out as danced out' (Macquarrie, 1971, p. 212). This leads to the conclusion that it 'is awe, then, that constitutes the core of the primitive religious consciousness, and is man's reaction to the hidden mysterious forces of his environment' (pp. 212f.). There is here, as Eric Sharpe observes, a tendency 'to regard religion as having developed in the depths of the individual mind as a result of a peculiar reflective process, in which 'experiences' had played a large part' (1986, p. 70).

Foundations of Psychological Research

In terms of research into spiritual development by far the most significant example of this tendency to give priority to experience is encountered in the work of William James (1842–1910). His *Varieties of Religious Experience* constitutes the first classic empirical psychological investigation of religious experience (James, 1960). James approaches religious experience as a natural phenomenon, and presents evidence of how religious people utilise such experience as a means of transcending the empirical world and engaging with the realm of the divine or transcendent. For James his research into religious experience provides 'empirical confirmation for the religious hypothesis – the hypothesis that our lives are continuous with a larger spiritual world' (Macquarrie, 1971, p. 178). Though James' work was soon eclipsed by the rise of forms of psychoanalysis and behaviourist psychology generally suspicious of such claims, in retrospect it can be seen to have provided the foundation for the exploration of children's spirituality that flourished in the latter third of the twentieth century.

Manifestation in Spiritual Education

The preference for a phenomenology of manifestation over a hermeneutic of proclamation also reflects the mainstream opinion of the majority of contemporary spiritual educators who are quick to draw attention to 'the neglect of interpretations of spiritual awareness which would highlight the role played by emotion and forms of experience not confined to our rational cognitive capacities' (Hay *et al.*, 1996, p. 48).

Investigating the Spiritual Lives of Children

In the mid-1960s the zoologist Alistair Hardy, responding to the comparative failure to build on James' pioneering study of the phenomenon of religious experience, established the Religious Experience Research Unit at Manchester College in Oxford. The unit gathered together over 4,000 first-hand accounts by adults of significant religious and spiritual experience. Two of Hardy's publications, *The Divine Flame* and *The Spiritual Nature of Man* quickly attained the status of contemporary classics in the field (Hardy 1966, 1979).

Hardy was deeply impressed by the range and depth of reported experiences of key moments of heightened emotion and spiritual awareness, and moved quickly to the conclusion that he was faced with a form of transcendent insight significantly different from our ordinary everyday experience. The collected evidence demonstrated to Hardy that a significant number of individuals in contemporary society are aware of the presence in their lives of some form of transcendent being or power despite modern scepticism regarding such a reality.

The consensus of opinion prior to Hardy's work was that religious experience was best accounted for reductively. The tradition of psychoanalysis tended to explain away religious experience as an expression of unconscious desire, while behaviourist psychology sought to interpret it in terms of immanent biological causation. Such reductionist accounts of the phenomenon did not require the hypothesis of a transcendent reality, but instead pointed 'toward belief in subconscious motivation on the one hand, and toward a refined form of mental engineering on the other' (Sharpe, 1986, p. 98).

Hardy set out to actively resist both the psychoanalytic and determinist schools of thought. Spiritual experience he claimed – in the face of psychoanalytic opposition – is experience of an actual objective reality, and as such cannot be dismissed as mere illusion: far from being a pathological aberration, religious experience is natural to the human condition, an integral part of our normal biological make-up. Against behaviourist psychology he argued that our biological make-up does not constitute a reductive *cause* of our spiritual experience, but rather that we possess a biologically determined *openness* to transcendent reality. Consequently, Hardy came to see his research as challenging the modern hermeneutic of suspicion directed against objective spiritual reality. The evidence was clear: human beings are spiritual by nature.

The extent of the available evidence suggested to Hardy that he was dealing with a universal reality that transcends specific religious traditions and doctrines. This led him to adopt an experiential–expressive model of religion, and view religious experience as the foundation of all religious culture. As Hay points out, 'from Hardy's perspective, the many religions of *Homo Sapiens* are the richly varied cultural responses of human beings to their natural spiritual awareness' (Hay and Nye, 1998, p. 10). Since such experience could clearly manifest itself apart from any specific religious context, there was no necessary connection between spiritual experience and religion. 'On Hardy's thesis, spirituality is not the exclusive property of any one religion, or for that matter of religion in general' (ibid., p. 11).

Though Hardy's research was confined to reports provided by adults, it prepared the ground for the extension of his work into the field of the spirituality of childhood. 'The implication of taking Hardy's view seriously for an understanding of children's spirituality is considerable because it implies that there is in every child a spiritual potentiality no matter what the child's cultural context may be' (Hay *et al.*, 1996, p. 61). It was Hardy's successor as director of the Religious Experience Research Unit, Edward Robinson, who established children's spirituality as a key issue in contemporary research.

The Original Vision: A Study of the Religious Experience of Childhood, was the result of Robinson's recognition that many of the accounts of religious experience gathered by the unit frequently drew on childhood reminiscences (Robinson, 1977). These recollections attested to the vitality of childhood experience, and affirmed its significance in shaping personal identity and providing a sense of meaning and purpose in life.

It became clear to Robinson as he analysed the reports that many of the religious experiences of childhood were of lasting significance, playing an important role in the transition to adult life. However, he also recognised the possibility that this primal vision could be displaced during the transition to adulthood, and consequently undermined and repressed by the demands of adult life. There could be no automatic guarantee that the purity of the child's original vision would achieve maturity in adulthood.

This led Robinson to challenge the prevailing paradigm of child development, as represented by Ronald Goldman's model of the cognitive development of religious language. Goldman had rejected the significance of spiritual and mystical experience in childhood. 'The mystics who claim to have direct sensations of the divine,' he claimed, 'are extremely rare cases, rarer in adolescence and practically unknown in childhood' (Goldman 1964, p. 14; Hay and Nye, 1998, p. 41). Instead he offered a model rooted in children's evolving capacity for religious and moral reasoning. This stress on the intellectual over against the emotive was, for Robinson, an example of how adults could unwittingly undermine the original vision of childhood.

Activity

The first approach to a spiritual experience which I can remember must have taken place when I was five or six years old at the house where I was born and brought up. It was a calm, limpid summer morning and the early mist still lay in wispy wreaths among the valleys. The dew on the grass seemed to sparkle like irridescent (sic) jewels in the sunlight, and the shadows of the houses and trees seemed friendly and protective. In the heart of the child that I was there suddenly seemed to well up a deep and overwhelming sense of gratitude, a sense of unending peace and security which seemed to be part of the beauty of the morning, the love and protective and living presence which included all that I had ever loved and yet was something much more.

(Robinson, 1977, p. 33)

- How do you react to this example of childhood religious experience as reported by Robinson? A profound engagement with the ultimate meaning of life? Or sugar-coated sentimentality?
- Can you recall any key childhood experiences that helped shape your own identity? Does Robinson's framework of interpretation do justice to them?

Robinson perceived the need for a much greater level of sensitivity towards the actual experience of children, and a far greater reticence in imposing on them any restrictive intellectual framework. With this caution in mind, he draws a number of conclusions regarding this 'original vision', a vision which is:

- no mere imaginative fantasy, but a form of knowledge essential for human maturity;
- related to some form of transcendent or mystical experience;
- only properly understood reflectively, in the transition from childhood to adulthood;
- self-authenticating, possessing its own absolute authority;
- purposive, crucial for identity formation and a sense of purpose, destiny or fate;
- essentially religious.

Robinson, of course, was entirely dependent on adult recollections of childhood. The obvious next step in the research process was to focus on children themselves. The last thirty years has seen a remarkable growth of such studies. An outstanding example is Robert Cole's *The Spiritual Life of Children* (1992), which presents a series of conversations with children gathered over an extended period of time and crossing cultural and religious boundaries. His research does not attempt to impose any closed interpretative framework on the conversations, but instead seeks to allow children to present their ultimate concerns for themselves, in their own terms. The richness of Coles' work is impossible to encapsulate in a brief summary, and the reader is urged to read this book.

David Hay: The Children's Spirituality Project

Prior to his exploration of children's spirituality David Hay had already published research which revealed that 'spiritual experience is very widely reported in the adult population of Britain', and suggested 'the probability that about two thirds of the population are aware of a spiritual dimension to their experience' (Hay and Nye, 1998, p. 16). In addition, he had already played a significant role in helping to shape the pedagogic framework of contemporary spiritual education.

Locating his research firmly in the tradition of Hardy and Robinson, Hay accepts 'a notion of spirituality as something biologically built into the human species, an holistic awareness of reality which is potentially to be found in every human being' (ibid., p. 57). Like Hardy, he rejects reductionist accounts of spiritual experience, asserting instead that 'children's spirituality is rooted in a universal human awareness ... "really there" and not just culturally constructed illusion' (ibid., p. 4). He accepts that spiritual experience transcends religious and cultural boundaries, and that 'knowledge about religion and the ability to use religious language is not the whole story when we are thinking about spirituality' (ibid., p. 57). This in turn leads him to affirm the pre-linguistic experiential foundations of spiritual sensibility.

The exploration of adult spirituality conducted by Hay drew the conclusion that our openness to spiritual experience is in danger of being eroded by modern secular culture. The post-Enlightenment hermeneutic of suspicion serves to undermine and distort what is in fact an innate and natural capacity for spiritual awareness. This leads him to suggest that the erosion of spiritual sensibility may be less marked in children than in adults, since it is 'the process of induction into adult society (that) may more often than not have the effect of closing it down' (ibid., p. 20). Consequently, 'one might suppose that in contemporary culture spirituality would be more prominent in childhood than in adult life' (ibid.). Hay's research was from the start 'optimistic in the hope of discovering that children do still reach out towards that mystery which lies outside our control' (ibid., pp. 74f.).

Activity

> I want to argue that children's spirituality is rooted in a universal human awareness; that it is 'really there' and not just a culturally constructed illusion.
>
> (Hay and Nye, 1998, p. 4)

- Do you agree with Hay's assertion?
- What are the strengths and weaknesses of his position?
- Does it provide a viable basis for spiritual education in a pluralistic multi-cultural society?
- What alternative ways are there of making sense of the prevalence of childhood spiritual experience?

Hay's research begins by proposing a sketch-map of the terrain of children's spirituality. He argues that we need 'to learn to become at home in this landscape and used to the vocabulary and practices of children in their own exploration if we are to help to protect their spirituality' (ibid., pp. 58f). To this end he posits three core categories of spiritual sensitivity:

- *Awareness sensing* – This refers to the children's ability to attend to the here-and-now of experience and to get themselves in tune with life's ebb and flow. This involves openness to the possibility of achieving forward momentum as, for example, at the moment when the 'penny drops' and light is suddenly shed on an apparently irresolvable problem. Such awareness of the immediacy of experience takes the form of a holistic wisdom in which body and soul operate as one.
- *Mystery sensing* – Children's spirituality is assumed to be rooted in a sense of wonder and awe in the face of the inherent mystery of the universe, a sense open to stimulation through an active imagination.
- *Value sensing* – The ebb and flow of life, when illuminated by the mystery of life, will produce in children both delight and despair, and instil in them a capacity to respond to issues raised by questions of the ultimate goodness of the world and the ultimate meaning of life.

Rebecca Nye, in her contribution to Hay's research programme, identifies a common thread in their research data, present whenever researchers experienced 'an initial intuitive sense of children's spirituality' (ibid., p. 111). This is identified as 'the essence by which children's spirituality may be known', and 'became the "core category" of the theoretical framework' (ibid.). The heart of children's spirituality is labelled their 'relational consciousness', understood as 'an unusual level of consciousness or perceptiveness ... expressed in a context of how the child related to things, other people, him/herself, and God' (ibid., p. 113).

Hay's research, supported by the work of Nye, thus affirms that children possess an innate capacity for spiritual experience, a 'relational consciousness', rooted in an immediate awareness of the mystery and meaning of life, and concerned with children's sense of identity, their place in the world, in society, and in the ultimate order of things.

Clive Erricker: The Children and Worldviews Project

The Children and Worldviews Project departs from the presuppositions of Hardy, Robinson and Hay by adopting a post-modern perspective on children's spirituality (Erricker, *et al.*, 1997). For Clive Erricker, attempts to identify the essence of children's spirituality and posit an objective transcendent spiritual reality result in the construction of a meta-narrative which contains far too many rationalistic presuppositions. The nebulous nature of spirituality is assumed from the outset, and it is accepted that 'it is difficult to define the way in which children view their world' (ibid., p. 30). In accordance with a post-modern world-view, it is assumed that human beings are both highly complex and in a constant state of flux, so that 'what is true about them today may not be true tomorrow' (ibid., p. 31). Like Hay, Erricker identifies a 'social context where normal spiritual or religious language is either absent or suppressed or repressed because of problems of plausibility in modern scientific culture.' (Hay *et al.*, 1996, p. 63). However, Erricker's conclusions are far more radical than those of Hay, ruling out the possibility of identifying an immutable biological essence of children's spirituality. This is not to suggest that research cannot come up with rigorous and valid results, but it is to say that any such results will throw more light on the distinctive spiritual experiences of individual children than on any supposed universal core of children's spirituality.

Activity

> I remember when my mum and Dad split up I was very upset becaus my mum throw a shoe at my dad and take a chunk of skin out of dads face I still cry when my and mum met mum gets very upset so she always takes my out alote to stop he cry and get her mid of this. Please read this (sic.).
>
> (Erricker *et al.*, 1997, p. 97)

Erricker's research frequently digs down to the raw nerve of children's spiritual experience and encounters primal experiences of pain, suffering and loss.

- Is such experience an appropriate topic for classroom discussion?
- What reasons can you give for supporting a sensitive engagement with such issues in the classroom?
- What reasons are there for avoiding such issues? Is a genuine spiritual education that engages directly with issues of the ultimate meaning of life a practical possibility?

Spirituality and Education

Erricker's research targets are clearly stated: 'We wanted to know what children felt was important in their lives … what coloured the way they looked at the world' (Erricker *et al.*, 1997, p. 34). The adopted research strategy – of qualitative open-ended grounded research carried out through unstructured group interviews – deliberately sets out to be sensitive enough to respond to the rich diversity of children's spiritual lives. Enormous effort is put into ensuring that the researcher acknowledges and respects the unique identity of each individual child and avoids the danger of forcing their responses into any preconceived interpretative framework. The task is to find ways of 'allowing the children space and time in which to express themselves freely and without the hindrance of us as adults presuming to give them the appropriate tools and language' (ibid., p. 35).

The research findings published to date report children's responses to issues such as conflict and loss, parental separation, religious and scientific thinking, and ethnic and religious identity. Despite the stress on the uniqueness of the individual, it is possible to draw some general conclusions from the data.

Range, Breadth and Depth

Though Erricker and his colleagues anticipated that children would have a rich vein of stories to draw on, they 'were surprised about the number of children who communicated deep-seated hopes, fears and concerns about their experiences', and note the large number of children interviewed 'dealing with lives fragmented by loss and conflict' (Erricker *et al.*, 1997, p. 60).

Language and Explanation

Children were found to have 'developed quite complex explanations of their experiences with reference to enabling concepts onto which they had placed their own interpretations', and displayed an ability to 'construct or utilise metaphorical language consciously or unconsciously in order to explain what would otherwise have been incommunicable' (ibid., pp. 60f.).

Imagination

The use of metaphor and story to respond to the experiences life threw at them was grounded in a surprisingly rich imagination, coupled with significant levels of affective thinking and emotional intelligence. 'We did not expect that their imaginations would be used to such serious purpose in coping with difficulties arising through loss and separation' (ibid., p. 60). Consequently, children need 'to be enabled to express and reflect on learning derived from experience and imagination' (ibid., p. 136).

Identity and Meaning

Children's imagination was found to be purposeful, seeking to establish and maintain a sense of identity and meaning. 'Image and symbol, ritual and play were of great importance in the way that children constructed and maintained the most important aspects of their world-views' (ibid., p. 61).

Dissonance

Many of the children interviewed displayed enormous moral and spiritual maturity in responding to situations of conflict. Though they were often capable of resolving dissonance in their lives, and wished to accept personal responsibility for this, they often reported a lack of adult interest and support.

Need and Willingness to Communicate

The researchers regularly comment on their experience of children's willingness to 'trust outsiders with powerful and secret stories which were private to them' (ibid., p. 60). They detect in this an often unfulfilled need to talk through experiences with trustworthy adults.

Adult Facilitation

At they same time – and, at first glance at least, in apparent tension with Hay's hypothesis of the cultural erosion of spiritual experience – the research identified the important role that adults could, and occasionally did, play in supporting and guiding the emergence of a coherent world-view. The nurture of families and religious communities was found to be particularly significant in this respect.

Some Implications of the Research

There can be little doubt that the work of Robinson, Hay and Erricker exemplifies a growing body of evidence attesting to the rich and complex spiritual lives of children. The research evidence shows beyond a shadow of doubt that if we accept that spirituality is intricately bound up with concern for the ultimate meaning and purpose of life, then the vast majority of children enjoy rich and challenging spiritual lives that are at the centre of their developing self-understanding. It is clear that any serious spiritual pedagogy must attend to this evidence.

However, any more precise conclusions which might be drawn from the research remain matters of dispute. While the data support suggestions that modern culture serves to erode the reality of children's spiritual sensibility, particularly as they develop into adulthood, they also tend to confirm the positive role played by individuals and communities in establishing and nurturing children towards spiritual maturity. Research has yet to fully illuminate the positive and negative functions of socialisation and education on children's spiritual development.

A similar ambiguity surrounds the precise nature and status of spiritual experience, and of any transcendent reality to which such experience might be linked. The data raise, but do not solve, the question of the relationship between 'ultimate concern' and 'ultimate truth'. While Robinson and Hay follow Hardy in drawing clear theological conclusions about a natural capacity for spiritual sensibility and the existence of an objective spiritual reality underpinning spiritual experience, Erricker is far less quick to draw such essentialist conclusions, preferring instead to concentrate on the unclassified existential experience of individual children.

Nicholas Lash has responded critically to Hardy's assumption, itself reflecting the earlier work of William James, of an in-built biological propensity for spiritual experience: 'It is perhaps more disturbing in 1980, than it was in 1900, to find a scientist of distinction offering such detailed descriptions without a trace of what we might call hermeneutical curiosity' (Lash, 1988, p. 98). Lash here is drawing attention to a tendency to draw premature philosophical and theological conclusions from the research data. In doing so he identifies a widespread problem with the research. Lash invites us towards a more circumspect and cautious response: the reality of a depth and richness of children's grappling with ultimate spiritual questions is unavoidable, but the implications for our understanding of the nature and source of their experience, of the social and communal forces at work, and of the implications for educational policy and practice, remain a matter for debate.

Summary

- Exploration of children's spiritual experience, which generally assumes an experiential–expressive model of religion, has had a profound influence on the policy and practice of spiritual education.
- Key stages in the history of the development of the research are reflected in the work of Robinson, Hay and Erricker.
- The universality and vitality of children's spiritual experience, and its role in shaping their identities and leading them to grapple with ultimate questions of meaning and purpose, are of fundamental significance for the task of spiritual education.
- In revealing children's vital experiential engagement with questions of ultimate meaning and truth, psychological research demonstrates the ongoing significance of the complex maze of philosophical and religious options explored in the previous two chapters, but does not necessarily take us any further in our attempts to navigate a path through it.

5 The Social Dimension of Spirituality

The excursions into the realms of philosophy, theology and psychology in the preceding chapters have shed light on the complex nature of spirituality and on its continuing significance for personal and communal growth. It is increasingly clear, given the plurality of spiritual attitudes and beliefs, that any adequate pedagogy will have to treat spirituality as a controversial subject. At the same time the inherent ambiguity of spirituality serves to reinforce a growing sense of the vital importance of an informed encounter with questions of life's ultimate meaning and purpose.

The final task in Part I of this study is to use the insights of sociology to develop a picture of the rich tapestry of spiritual attitudes and beliefs encountered in contemporary British society. An investigation of the phenomenon of secularisation leads into an overview of the spiritual landscape of Britain. The various forms of spirituality associated with adherents to organised religion, secular atheists and those whose spiritual positions are best characterised as 'believing without belonging' are then explored in greater depth. The chapter finally takes the opportunity to draw a number of broad conclusions from the exploration of the nature and scope of spirituality carried out in Part I, thereby providing a bridge to the exploration of contemporary spiritual education in Part II.

The Theory of Secularisation

Central to any attempt to understand the social landscape of contemporary spirituality must be the recognition that we live in a predominantly secular society. It was Auguste Comte (1798–1857), one of the founders of the discipline of sociology and a leading figure in the positivist tradition of French sociology, who first articulated the theory of secularisation. Comte believed that empirical observation, modelled on the methodology of the natural sciences, can provide us with a rational account of society. He suggested that civilisation has passed through three distinct stages:

1   a *theological stage*, in which events are attributed to the actions of gods, demons and spirits;
2   a *metaphysical stage*, in which reality is explained through philosophical ideas such as essence, substance and being;

3   a *positivistic* stage, in which the world is described using the principles of empir-
    ical science.

On the basis of this evolutionary model Comte concluded that religious belief is an
implausible hypothesis, and that religion is consequently in a process of terminal
decline. Comte's theory has trickled down into popular consciousness, giving rise to
the commonly encountered sentiment that religious belief is little more than
outmoded superstition.

'Secularisation' is used as a technical term in sociological literature to refer to
'those processes by which religion loses its dominance or social significance in
society' (Northcott, 1999, p. 214). There is a wealth of evidence to support the
claim that Britain is an increasingly secular society. Levels of church going, for
example, have declined dramatically in the last hundred years, and the percentage of
the nation's children baptised in the Church of England has slipped from 70 per cent
before the Second World War to as little as 25 per cent in 1977 (ibid., p. 215). A
range of studies have drawn attention to the 'drift from the churches during childhood and adolescence', and to the fact that 'the drift has accelerated since the early
1970s into the 1990s' (Kay and Francis, 1996, p. 141).

Despite such evidence Comte's secularisation thesis has, in recent years, been
subject to significant revision. Many sociologists now prefer to talk in terms of a
fundamental re-orientation of the nation's religious beliefs and practices rather than
of their inevitable decline and disappearance.

A key mark of secularisation is the withdrawal of religious influence in the public
domain. This is visible in the declining membership of religious communities, in the
decrease of religious practice, in the fading of the influence of religious influence on
social life, politics and public affairs, and in the eclipse of the authority of Christian
doctrinal and moral teaching. However, sociologists are becoming increasingly
aware that this has not led, as Comte predicted, to the terminal decline of religion,
but instead to a widespread re-location of religious life in the private sphere of
personal belief and piety. This view is supported by the psychological evidence
presented in the last chapter, which suggested that personal religious and spiritual
experience continues to flourish despite the decline of religion in the public arena.

'From Cathedrals to Cults'

Steve Bruce, in his book *Religion in the Modern World: From Cathedrals to Cults*
(1996), has developed a defence of the secularisation thesis that takes into account
the persistence of religious belief. He begins by tracing the roots of secularisation
back to the sixteenth-century European Reformation. The importance placed by
the Protestant Reformers on personal faith, he suggests, produced a culture of individualism that undermined the communal foundations of religion. At the same time
their rejection of medieval religious superstition and affirmation of the importance
of reflective faith gave birth to rational ways of thinking that placed a question
mark over the plausibility of religious belief. These trends came to a head in
the Enlightenment's insistence on the importance of human autonomy and rationality and gave birth to modern religious scepticism. Though the foundations of

secularisation were established several centuries ago, the transition to a secular society has been a slow one. Bruce suggests that this is due to the narrow parochial lives enjoyed by most of the population prior to the advent of mass communication, and the inherent – though now rapidly declining – strength of the political and social power-base of the conservative Christian establishment.

Bruce argues that the nineteenth century was a time of 'serial dogmatism'. By this he means that the battle for the religious hearts and minds of the nation was played out within the confines of the various Christian denominations. Shifts in religious allegiance did not, generally speaking, include the option of embracing atheism, agnosticism, or any of the non-Christian religious traditions. Instead individuals shifted their commitments from one Christian tradition to another, with Anglicans, Roman Catholics, Baptists, Methodists, Presbyterians and a host of other independent Protestant churches and sects battling amongst themselves for the spiritual allegiance of the population.

When the twin forces of individualism and rationalism finally came into their own in the twentieth century the result was a shift from 'serial dogmatism' to 'promiscuous liberalism'. The possibility of shifting religious allegiance now embraced the possibilities of atheism, agnosticism, non-Christian religious traditions, a variety of new religious movements, and private forms of piety and spirituality. At the same time the crossing of religious boundaries achieved levels of social acceptability unimaginable in previous centuries. Consequently society gradually became marked by post-modern religious eclecticism in which 'the diminishing number of people who continue to do religion do it in an increasingly individualistic and idiosyncratic manner' (Bruce, 1996, p. 233). Now, 'instead of religiosity expressing itself in new sects with enthusiastic believers, it is expressed through piecemeal and consumerist involvement in elements of a cultic world' (ibid., p. 234).

Activity

- To what extent does the revised theory of secularisation, as presented by Bruce, coincide with your own experience of the changing nature of belief in contemporary Britain?
- In your experience, are the plausibility structures of religion being eroded or relocated in the private sphere?
- Do the range of attitudes and beliefs represented in your school as a whole, including staff, pupils and parents, reflect a widespread process of secularisation?
- Is there evidence in your educational community for the persistence of religious belief in a privatised form?
- Are you able to identify a flourishing attitude of post-modern 'promiscuous liberalism' in the way sections of the school community respond towards issues of core beliefs and values?

Crucially, Bruce rejects Comte's belief that the plausibility structure of religion has been eradicated, and that current manifestations of religion are nothing more than the remnants of outmoded and irrational world-views. The decline in the popularity of institutional religion

> does not suppose that patently false superstitions will be replaced by patently obvious truth as people become better educated or that modern people will become self-consciously committed to an atheistic and materialistic view of themselves and the universe.
>
> (ibid., p. 234)

The re-location of religion in the private sphere reflects the persistence of faith, while at the same time making it increasingly difficult for many to respond appropriately to spiritual experience.

> Like the truly tone-deaf, we know about music, we know that many people feel strongly about it, we might even be persuaded that, in some social sense, it is a good thing, but still it means nothing to us.
>
> (ibid., p. 234)

The Landscape of Belief

To what extent does the empirical evidence support Bruce's thesis? The process of placing figures on aspects of religious belief and practice is notoriously difficult and controversial. However, the evidence gathered in Grace Davie's monograph *Religion in Britain Since 1945: Believing Without Belonging* (1994), allows us to identify the basic trends. In the interests of clarity I have taken the liberty of rounding Davie's figures to the nearest percentage point, and elected not to repeatedly labour the point that all such figures are approximate.

Membership of Religious Communities

At first glance the evidence regarding religious community membership appears to contradict the notion that we live in a predominantly secular and pluralistic society. About 71 per cent of the British population claim membership of a religious community. Of these, 64 per cent belong to one of the mainstream Christian churches, and 7 per cent adhere to either sectarian offshoots of Christianity, or a non-Christian religious tradition. Of the approximately 37.6 million Christians in the country 26.7 million are Anglican, 5.6 million are Roman Catholic, and the remaining 5.3 million are distributed between the Baptist, Independent, Methodist, Orthodox, Pentecostal and Presbyterian denominations. Of the 3.7 million members of non-Christian communities, 1.1 are Muslim, 0.6 belong to post-Christian off-shoots of Christianity, 0.6 are Sikh, 0.4 Hindu, 0.4 Scientologists, 0.3 Jewish, and 0.3 belong to other religious traditions.

Extent of Regular Religious Practice

However, the reality of secularisation manifests itself when the question of communal membership is replaced by that of the extent of regular religious practice. Taking the population as a whole we find that 29 per cent claim no allegiance to a religious community and consequently do not take part in any form of religious practice, 56 per cent are non-practising members of a religious community, and only 15 per cent claim to practise their religion on a regular basis. Religion, it would seem, continues to have a hold on the majority of the population, but this hold is little more than nominal. It appears to be convenient for the majority to retain an identification with a religious tradition, but that such identification does not lead them to any significant level of active involvement in the community.

Persistence of Personal Religious Belief

However perhaps the most significant factor in our exploration of the contours of contemporary belief in Britain emerges when a third question is asked, not of community membership or public practice, but of personal religious belief and private religious practice. The evidence provides much food for thought: 72 per cent of the population believe in God, 63 per cent see themselves as being religious people, 60 per cent pray in private on a regular basis, and 52 per cent report that God is important in their lives. The remarkably high levels of nominal community membership parallel evidence of extensive levels of private belief and practice, and both contrast strongly with the significantly low levels of public practice. This situation is admirably summed up in the sub-title of Davie's book: we are a nation that believes but does not belong.

What is the significance of all this for our understanding of the landscape of British spirituality? Broadly speaking, in it we can identify three main groupings.

1 Organised religion – the 15 per cent of the population who embrace spiritual traditions grounded in membership of a variety of religious communities.
2 Atheism – the 29 per cent of the population who embrace forms of spirituality shaped by the rejection of religion.
3 'Believing without Belonging' – the 56 per cent of the population who approach spirituality via a continuing private commitment to the importance of the spiritual dimension of their lives, despite only nominal allegiance to religious communities.

Activity

- To what extent are the broad proportions of (i) 15 per cent active membership of a religious community; (ii) 29 per cent practical atheism; and (iii) 56 per cent 'believing without belonging' reflected in your school community?
- Are there ways in which you would wish to reformulate this picture?

Organised Religion

Organised religion occupies a significant, if increasingly marginal, place in the landscape of contemporary spirituality. Regardless of question marks over the plausibility of religious belief, formalised religion clearly continues to offer 'certain crucial psychological and social functions including the provision of individual meaning and life-purpose, explanations of suffering, and moral values and procedures' (Northcott, 1999, p. 197). In assessing the spiritual significance of organised religion it is important to develop a realistic perspective.

Viewed from a global perspective, the experience of organised religion in Britain is a parochial local one from which it is inappropriate to draw universal conclusions. The experience of widespread institutional decline is not repeated elsewhere in the world. Many religions have experienced significant global expansion during the present century, and areas of the United States enjoy levels of participation in organised religion significantly higher than in Europe. This is especially significant as education increasingly develops perspectives that transcend national boundaries.

It is equally important to resist the danger of idealising Britain's religious past. Robin Gill has argued, in *The Myth of the Empty Church* (1993), that 'the extent of churchgoing decline in England has been exaggerated as a consequence of the over-building of churches by the Victorians' (Northcott, 1999, p. 207). This raises the possibility that current perceptions of religious decline have been exaggerated by a misplaced vision of a past golden age of British religious history in which committed and regular church going is assumed to have been a national norm.

The phenomenological description of religion practised in departments of Religious Studies has tended to produce idealised versions of the world's major religious traditions. They are presented in essentialist terms as tightly structured edifices with clear creeds, stable practices and clearly delineated boundaries. The recent rise of interest in ethnographic studies has shown grass-roots religion to be much more fluid in nature, continuously developing and changing in the light of their internal tensions and external pressures, subject to doxological eclecticism, doctrinal heterodoxy, diverse levels and forms of commitment, significant levels of manoeuvrability within and between communities, and loose and even invisible boundaries between traditions.

The Diversification of Christianity

About 64 per cent of the population claim at least nominal allegiance to Christianity, making it by far the most numerically significant of the world's religious traditions currently represented in Britain. With the growth of the ecumenical movement traditional denominational divisions within Christianity play less of a dominant role than previously. Whether you are Baptist, Methodist, Roman Catholic or Anglican is now generally less important than whether you identify with the catholic, evangelical, charismatic, liberal or radical wings of the church. Levels of commitment and styles of spirituality are increasingly more significant than group adherence. Among the ongoing tensions within Christianity probably the most important is the degree of engagement with, or resistance to, modern culture. It is generally Evangelical and Pentecostal forms of piety that show greatest resistance to decline, and even an openness to growth, a situation best explained by 'the capacity of conservative congregations and churches to maintain boundaries of meaning and commitment, distinguishing their doctrinal beliefs and moral values and lifestyles from the dominant culture' (Northcott, 1999, p. 197).

The Emergence of World Faiths

Despite the existence of a long-standing and established national church, Britain has never been an exclusively Christian country. In the middle ages the Church adopted strategies ranging from assimilation through tolerance to persecution in its relationships with indigenous paganism, the Jewish Diaspora, and (what it perceived to be) the external 'threat' of Islam. However, energy was eventually directed towards internal tensions, with the Church of England – itself a mixture of catholic, liberal and evangelical spirituality – seeking to hold the middle ground against the 'extremes' of Roman Catholicism and Protestant non-conformity. The 1950s and 1960s saw the massive influx of world faiths into Britain, producing what is now the rich multi-faith kaleidoscope of contemporary British religion. These world faiths were introduced by a mixture of immigrants seeking employment and refugees fleeing persecution. The ranks of the long-established Anglo-Jewish community were swelled by European Jews fleeing persecution. Muslims migrated from Bangladesh, Pakistan and India, and later from Cyprus and Uganda. Indians from Gujarat and the Punjab brought with them Hinduism and Sikhism.

The Growth of New Religious Movements

Alongside the diversification of Christianity and growth of the major world faiths Britain has also witnessed a rapid expansion in the number and range of New Religious Movements in recent years. Amongst the most significant of these are the Unification Church, the Church of Scientology and the International Society for Krishna Consciousness. Though numerically insignificant, their adherents add to the complex tapestry of organised religions constituting a vibrant dimension of British spirituality (Saliba, 1995).

Atheism

What of the self-proclaimed religiously tone-deaf? Those who, whether consciously or by default, reject both formal and informal religion in favour of forms of practical atheism? It is a fundamental mistake to assume that the displacement of religion brings with it a parallel displacement of spirituality. Neither the atheist teacher nor the atheist pupil can legitimately claim to be able to side-line spirituality. On the contrary, the rejection of God makes the question of the ultimate meaning and purpose of life all the more significant. For the atheist spiritual answers are to be found in the immanent world of nature, rather than in an imaginary transcendent realm populated by divine beings. Atheism, just like religion, is capable of drawing into its fold types of spirituality ranging from the sublime to the ridiculous. The profound insights of the tradition of atheistic Humanism stand alongside an atheistic fundamentalism typified by a hedonistic consumerism driven by emotional and physical gratification.

Activity

Throughout this book it is assumed that spirituality cannot be confined to the domain of religion, but embraces all human experience, including that of atheists. Clearly, such an assumption is crucial for the future development of spiritual pedagogy.

- Is the assumption of the universal nature of spirituality justifiable?
- Or does it merely represent a rearguard attempt to justify a form of education that ought to have no place in the school curriculum?

What is the ultimate meaning of life in a Godless universe? The spiritual responses to this question are complex and diverse: nihilism, cynicism and despair; consumerism; physical health and mental well-being; technological control of the environment; attentive respect for the environment; an Epicurean search for personal happiness; a utilitarian striving for the happiness of the majority; the pragmatic desire to protect the needs of the disenfranchised; an altruistic concern for the needs of the other; a humanistic striving to establish the liberal ideals of freedom, tolerance and reason.

Generally, atheists tend to avoid formal organisation, though the National Secular Society and British Humanist Association are significant exceptions. Nevertheless Humanist organisations do provide us with helpful lenses through which the spiritual implications of atheism can be clarified. Humanists, according to the British Humanist Association:

> think that this world and this life are all we have; that we should try to live full and happy lives ourselves and, as part of this, make it easier for other people to do the same; that all situations and people deserve to be judged on their merits by standards of reason and humanity; that individuality and social co-operation are equally important.
>
> (BHA, 1999)

The National Secular Society has been at the forefront of seeking to replace religious worship with humanistic celebrations of our common humanity through non-religious weddings, funerals and naming ceremonies. As a campaigning organisation its spiritual resources are directed towards improving the quality of human life. Amongst its causes it lists the abolition of the blasphemy laws, opposition to religious schooling in general and religious education in particular, advocacy of birth control, legal abortion and voluntary euthanasia, protection of minority rights, racial and sexual equality, freedom of speech and expression and animal welfare (NSC, 2000).

'Believing Without Belonging'

Davie has identified the emergence of the phenomena of 'believing without belonging' as among the most significant spiritual paradigm shifts in the modern world. Believers who don't actively belong to formalised religion accept the privatisation of spirituality and its dislocation from public religious life. If their concern for inner private spirituality reflects the philosophy of romanticism, the diversity of manifestations of such privatised spirituality is distinctively post-modern in form. The phenomenon of 'believing without belonging' is eclectic and extremely difficult to categorise. The middle-class executive disillusioned with her local parish church but drawing spiritual inspiration from BBC's *Songs of Praise*, and the New Age practitioner of an alternative culture rooted in astrology, faith healing and divination, are – despite their significant differences – participants in the same complex phenomena. Both have little faith in organised religion, both reject the option of atheism, and both are searching for some form of transcendental spiritual reality.

Here we will concentrate on the New Age Movement as an example of 'believing without belonging'. This does not imply any simple equation of New Age thought and practice and the broader phenomenon we are concerned with here. However, the increasingly high levels of diffusion of New Age themes and practices within popular culture make it a significant exemplar of the phenomenon, not least through its significant influence on some forms of contemporary spiritual education.

The New Age Movement is not to be confused with the various New Religious Movements, despite significant areas of cultural overlap. While the former is clearly resistant to any process of institutional formalisation, the latter can be seen to be a direct result of a desire to re-establish clearly differentiated religious communities. Paul Heelas identifies three main dimensions of New Age thinking:

1   *Cultural resistance* – from a New Age perspective modern culture represents *the* major threat to an authentic spiritual life:

    We malfunction because we have been indoctrinated – or, in the New Age sense of the term, been 'brainwashed' – by mainstream society and culture … To live in terms of [the mores of the established order] inculcated by parents, the educational system and other institutions, is to remain the victim of unnatural, deterministic and misguided routines.

    (Heelas, 1996, p. 18)

2   *Routes to perfection* – followers of New Age thinking seek to escape from the mores of modern culture by turning inwards, trusting their own authentic experience, and searching for personal perfection. 'The inner realm and the inner realm alone, is held to serve as the source of authentic vitality, creativity, love, tranquillity, wisdom, power, authority and all those other qualities which are held to compromise the perfect life' (ibid., p. 19).

3   *Techniques of salvation* – such inner spiritual awakening is made possible through a variety of spiritual techniques ranging from meditation and aroma therapy through to the use of hallucinogenic drugs and shamanic practices.

Heelas interprets the New Age Movement as an essentially counter-cultural movement within modernism. On the one hand, it responds to the uncertainties of modernity by providing counter-cultural conceptual tools and techniques which are able to secure and affirm a sense of personal identity. Yet at the same time many of its core assumptions are also found 'in that capitalistic heartland of modernity, namely the enterprise culture of Thatcherism and Reaganism' (1996. p. 154). Northcott's characterisation of the New Age movement as inextricably bound up with the cultural norms of late capitalism, may also be taken as a characterisation of the entire phenomena of 'believing without belonging'.

> New Age practices and beliefs may also be seen as religious responses to the stress, alienation and meaninglessness which are common experiences in advanced industrial societies, and yet responses which are culturally well adapted to modern consumer culture. ... New Age entrepreneuralism, with its spiritual pot pourri, reinvents ancient beliefs, therapies and manipulations of the spirit world in the archetypal modern capitalist modes of consumer choice and monetary exchanges.
>
> (Northcott, 1999, p. 204)

Summary

This chapter presented a sociological sketch of spirituality in contemporary Britain arguing for the existence of a mainstream of eclectic 'believing with belonging' flanked by the persistence of practical atheism on the one hand, and public religious practice on the other. Read in the light of previous chapters in Part I, it enables us to draw some provisional conclusions about the nature of spirituality in contemporary Britain.

Activity

Part I has attempted to describe the main contours of spirituality in contemporary Britain, drawing on the resources of philosophy, theology, psychology and sociology.

Before moving on to Part II take a few moments to review the main arguments presented in Chapters 1–5.

- Is it possible to draw the philosophical, theological, psychological and sociological perspectives into a coherent whole?
- Do they offer an acceptable picture of spirituality in contemporary Britain?
- Is the spiritual landscape described here reflected in your own school community?
- What do you understand to be the chief strengths and weaknesses of the picture sketched here?
- Are there ways in which you would choose to revise it?

The spiritual landscape is eclectic, complex and ambiguous, and this makes the quest for ultimate meaning and purpose in life all the more significant. While there is no adequate vantage point from which contemporary spirituality can be dissected and compartmentalised, four overlapping disciplines – philosophy, theology, psychology and sociology – offer windows into the current spiritual climate.

- *Philosophy* reveals a range of spiritual routes – materialism, romanticism, post-modernity and critical-realism – which throw light on the spiritual possibilities established by modern culture.
- *Theology* shows how the acceptance or rejection of religious belief opens up a range of spiritual options: atheism, theological orthodoxy, universalism and radicalism and various forms of religious and secular fundamentalism.
- *Psychology* throws light on the depth and breadth of spiritual experience in Britain today, and in doing so reinforces both the vital significance of spirituality for the well-being of humanity and the danger of drawing premature conclusions regarding the true nature of spirituality from reports of spiritual experience.
- *Sociology* highlights the diverse social contexts in which spirituality manifests itself in contemporary society, including the advance of atheism, the persistence and diversification of organised religion, to the rapid expansion of the phenomena of 'believing without belonging'.

It follows from all this that (i) the curriculum of spiritual education will need to find ways of adequately representing this spiritual diversity; (ii) the pedagogy of spiritual education will need to approach spirituality as a controversial issue; (iii) teachers of spiritual education will need to develop an appropriate understanding of their subject and be able to locate themselves within the contemporary spiritual land-scape.

Part II

Contemporary Spiritual Education

6 Historical Development

Part I of this study deliberately avoided any premature engagement with spiritual education itself, electing instead to explore more general issues of the nature and scope of spirituality and its place within society. This strategy was based on the judgement that the current malaise of spiritual education is inextricably linked with a failure to take account of the complex nature of spirituality. The previous chapters sought to begin to remedy this situation by sketching out the main contours of the landscape of contemporary spirituality. It quickly became clear that society is in the midst of a spiritual crisis caused by the failure to provide a viable solution to the question of the ultimate purpose and meaning of life. Our hunger for spiritual direction clashes head on with a diverse and seemingly impenetrable range of spiritual options. The resulting tensions invite a tired and often cynical withdrawal from informed engagement with spiritual questions, leading to significant levels of spiritual illiteracy. It is here that spiritual education – conceived as a means of enabling society to engage sensitively and intelligently with the ambiguous questions of spiritual value, meaning and truth – needs to come into its own. Associating spirituality with concern for the ultimate meaning and purpose of life, the philosophical, theological, psychological and sociological investigations in Part I drew two main conclusions: (i) that the question of the ultimate meaning and purpose of life is as vital now as it has ever been; and (ii) that the diverse range of spiritual options mark out spiritual as a controversial issue.

Against this background Part II offers a critical description of the contours of contemporary spiritual education. Chapter 6 presents a historical overview of the development of spiritual education and identifies a range of key issues currently facing the subject.

Chapter 7 explores two standard approaches to spiritual pedagogy: (i) *Inclusivism*, which sets out to establish a broad consensus within spiritual education, but ends up ignoring the essentially controversial nature of spirituality in favour of a bland uniformity; and (ii) *Exclusivism*, which attempts to overcome the problems inherent in the inclusive consensus by rooting spiritual education in one of a number of specific religious and secular spiritual traditions, only to fall into the trap of adopting indoctrinatory procedures.

Chapter 8 explores a liberal attempt to bypass the tensions between bland inclusivism and narrow exclusivism by introducing a critical dimension to the pedagogical process, an approach which, though flawed, points the way towards the model of critical spiritual education proposed in Part III.

Activity

- Review the spiritual education currently in place in your school, paying particular attention to the following:

    (i)   policy documents;
    (ii) management and leadership;
    (iii) school ethos;
    (iv) Collective Worship and/or school assembly;
    (v)   cross-curricular teaching;
    (vi) explicit spiritual education.

- To what extent does your school take seriously its duty to provide spiritual education for all pupils? Why is this?

The Critical Agenda

The main concern in Part II is to provide a critical overview of the current state of play in spiritual education. It develops the thesis that contemporary spiritual education has taken a wrong turn in electing to follow a paternalistic rather than a critical pedagogical strategy. Mainstream debate has centred on the choice of inducting pupils either into a vacuous all-inclusive model of spirituality or into one of a range of exclusive spiritual traditions. In both cases the essentially controversial nature of spirituality is effectively glossed over: inclusivism, in attempting to be acceptable to all, smoothes over the rough edges of spirituality, while the various versions of exclusivism, in proposing a single route through the terrain of spirituality, silence the voices of alternative traditions. Comparatively little attention is paid to the possibility of a critical pedagogy concerned to enable pupils to engage directly with the controversial nature of spirituality, thereby empowering them to live wisely and intelligently in a world marked by spiritual diversity and ambiguity.

Both inclusivism and exclusivism impose pre-packaged 'solutions' to the spiritual dilemma of contemporary society, and in doing so repeat pedagogical mistakes made by educators at the dawn of the modern era. Peter Gay, in his magisterial history of the Enlightenment, interprets the advent of modern education in terms of an alliance between (i) the desire to reform society and (ii) a commitment to individual freedom. He argues that political and social necessity effectively tore this alliance apart: 'with the overpowering presence of the illiterate masses and the absence of the habit of autonomy, freedom and reform were often incompatible' (Gay, 1973, p.497). As the need to stabilise society began to take precedence over the cultivation of individual autonomy, so schooling became an increasingly conservative means of social engineering. In turn this strategy blocked the emergence of a mature democratic society grounded in individual autonomy. The educators and philosophers of the Enlightenment found themselves led through the devious and embarrassing detours of repression and manipulation that were a denial and mockery of the world they hoped to bring into being: the very methods used to distribute the fruits of enlightenment seemed to be calculated to frustrate the Enlightenment itself.

(ibid.)

This pattern is currently repeating itself: (i) entirely legitimate concerns to avoid sectarian and socially divisive forms of spiritual education have resulted in the imposition of a bland inclusive common-denominator spirituality; (ii) equally legitimate concerns to avoid the danger of a spiritual vacuum at the heart of society have resulted in the imposition of a range of distinctive and exclusive spiritual traditions. Both approaches adopt paternalistic educational strategies that seek to paper over the cracks of our fragmented spiritual heritage, ignore its inherently controversial nature, and impose a pre-packaged solution to the current spiritual crisis. The result has been a dumbing-down of our children's spiritual insight, a failure to cultivate their capacity to respond sensitively and critically to questions of the ultimate meaning and purpose of life, and the eclipse of a critical spiritual education capable of producing viable levels of spiritual literacy.

Activity

- Are you able to identify a specific spiritual tradition – perhaps drawn from one or more of the philosophical, religious, psychological and sociological perspectives outlined in Part I – to which your school is committed?
- Does the spiritual education provided by your school do justice to the essentially controversial nature of the subject?
- To what extent can the spiritual pedagogy in your school be described as either 'paternalistic' or 'critical'?

The Collapse of the Christian Consensus in Education

The flowering of interest in spiritual education can be traced back to a speech made at Ruskin College in 1976 by Prime Minister James Callaghan. Inviting the nation to address the fundamental question 'What do the nation's schools exist for?', Callaghan effectively delivered the opening salvo in what became known as the 'Great Education Debate' (Callaghan, 1976). The very fact that the question of the nature of public education was raised at all reflected the ongoing fragmentation of the educational consensus rooted in the long-standing partnership between the state and the established Church of England (Chadwick, 1997; Copley, 1997).

This consensus has roots that can be traced back to the nineteenth century, and reached its peak in the 1944 Education Act. This legislation constituted a blueprint for the moral and spiritual rejuvenation of society in the aftermath of the horrors of the Second World War. The European Enlightenment's myth of progress, already dealt a terminal blow by the First World War, could not hope to survive the spiritual decay at the very heart of European civilisation, as illuminated by the horrors of Auschwitz, Belsen and Dachau. The mere cultivation of educated reason alone was not deemed sufficient for the rebuilding of civilised society, and so the state turned to the spiritual resources of the established Church of England, and of the nation's Christian heritage. The Church–State partnership consolidated by the Act promoted a dual system of Church and state-sponsored schools.

The Act made direct reference to spirituality: 'The statutory system of public education ... contributes towards the spiritual, moral, mental and physical development of the community' (HMSO, 1944, Pt. 2, Sec. 7). However, the core language employed was that of 'religion', with the inference that 'religion' referred exclusively to the 'Christian religion'. The spiritual dimension of education was confined within the narrow parameters of a confessional Christian education. Though an opt-out clause made provision for possible dissent on the part of both teachers and parents, the basis of the spiritual rejuvenation of society was to be found in the twin processes of Religious Education and Collective Worship. By teaching the basic doctrines of Christianity and nurturing pupils in the Christian virtues – especially as these appear in the Ten Commandments and the Sermon on the Mount – schools were to instil in the nation's children the norms of civilised Christian behaviour.

There was to be no engagement with alternative spiritual traditions, though the state did provide support for schools established by the Jewish and Roman Catholic communities. The only genuine dispute concerning the nature of spirituality surrounded the need to avoid denominational conflict between the various Protestant churches. Here education was to offer a common-denominator Protestant Christianity, without denominational bias.

The story of the decline of this Christian consensus is a complex one, and we must confine ourselves to highlighting three key factors:

1   *The eclipse of Christianity* – the 1960s saw an increasing recognition – especially among the ranks of the religious educators – that the assumption that Britain remained essentially a Christian country was no longer tenable. It was gradually accepted that the vast majority of children in schools were at best nominal Christians: 'believing without belonging', they possessed no more than a passing allegiance to the established Church. This did not lead immediately to the abandonment of the project of confessional Christian education. Instead it spurred efforts to rejuvenate Christian education through the pedagogical strategy of attempting to build conceptual and experiential bridges between the implicit life experiences of pupils and the explicit teachings of Christianity. However, by the mid-1970s this neo-confessionalism had been replaced with a modern multi-faith religious education concerned with the phenomenological description of religion rather than the process of induction into Christian belief.

2   *Developments in moral education* – the liberalisation of religious teaching was accompanied by a similar change in moral education. Focus shifted from the inculcation of norms of Christian behaviour, drawn from the Ten Commandments and the Sermon on the Mount, to a concern for the cultivation of a virtuous character based on the vision of liberal humanism. Pupils were schooled in the twin liberal virtues of freedom and tolerance as a means to establish common

cross-cultural understanding in a pluralistic society. The ultimate spiritual goal was no longer the transcendent truth of Christianity, but the establishment of a just, equitable and harmonious society. Ethical norms were increasingly based on the free moral decision of the child, rather than the authoritarian imposition of a Christian world-view. Increasingly, moral education encouraged children to make autonomous moral decisions through a process of values clarification, in which the teacher acted as neutral chairman in moral debate, while the Swann Report advocated the use of multi-faith Religious Education as a tool for enhancing social harmony (HMSO, 1985).

3 *The rise of progressive education* – without any significant change in legislation the Christian agenda of the 1944 Education Act was superseded in the 1970s by a moral and spiritual liberal humanism. Its concern to cultivate the twin processes of freedom and tolerance, rather than any concrete moral norms, drew charges of relativism, despite the non-negotiable nature of the liberal world-view. The priority given to the cultivation of character by the new moral education drew on the legacy of 1960s' progressive education. The shift from a subject-centred focus on curriculum content to a child-centred education concerned with rounded development of the whole child was accompanied by a call for education to be more directly relevant to the immediate needs of pupils. By the time of Callaghan's Ruskin speech the vanguard of educational progressivism was already being challenged by a resurgent traditionalism concerned to re-establish the basics of literacy and numeracy and a curriculum driven pedagogy. This desire to restore order, in the face of what was considered to be the self-imposed anarchy of progressivism, was to culminate in the legislation of 1988.

The collapse of the Christian consensus and the emergence of what appeared to many to be a relativistic moral education took place against the background of increasing tension between progressive and traditionalist visions of education. Education found itself in a state of crisis which occasioned Callaghan's 'Great Education Debate'. The question 'What are our schools for?', inevitably raised spiritual questions, since it was impossible to answer Callaghan's question without addressing the fundamental issue of the ultimate meaning and purpose of life.

The Establishment of Spiritual Education

Callaghan's Ruskin College speech was quickly followed by the Labour Government's Green Paper *Education in Our Schools*, which set out proposals for the establishment of a core curriculum and the articulation of a set of basic educational aims for schools in the state sector (DES, 1977). The first steps on the road to the 1988 Education Reform Act had been taken.

It was the contribution of Her Majesty's Inspectors to the debate, in their discussion paper *Curriculum 11–16*, which brought the issue of spirituality to the fore (DES/HMI, 1977a). The document argued that the primary aim of education should be to induct pupils into a set of key forms of knowledge: aesthetic and creative, ethical, linguistic, mathematical, physical, scientific, social and political, and spiritual.

In a supplement, responding to requests for clarification, HMI offered two contrasting definitions of spirituality (DES/HMI, 1977b). In doing so they established the fundamental tension between inclusive and exclusive approaches that continue to dominate current debate.

The first of these definitions was broadly anthropological in its focus, and clearly set out to be inclusive:

> The spiritual area is concerned with the awareness a person has of those elements in existence and experience which may be defined in terms of inner feelings and beliefs; they affect the way people see themselves and throw light for them on the purpose and meaning of life itself. Often these feelings and beliefs lead people to claim to know God and glimpse the transcendent; sometimes they represent that striving and longing for perfection which characterises human beings but always they are concerned with matters at the heart and root of existence.
>
> (DES/HMI, 1977b)

The second definition drew on theological categories, and the wording clearly betrays HMIs concern that such an overtly religious approach to spirituality ran the risk of being exclusive, acceptable only to a religious minority among the general public:

> The spiritual area is concerned with everything in human knowledge or experience that is connected with or derives from a sense of God or of gods. Spirituality is a meaningless adjective for the atheist and of dubious use to the agnostic. Irrespective of personal belief or disbelief, an unaccountable number of people have believed and do believe in the spiritual aspects of human life, and therefore their actions, attitudes and interpretations of events have been influenced accordingly.
>
> (ibid.)

In proposing a curriculum rooted in forms of knowledge HMI were building directly upon the educational philosophy of Paul Hirst. He advocated 'the idea of liberal education as a process concerned simply and directly with the pursuit of knowledge' (Hirst, 1965, p.114). The pursuit of knowledge 'was also conceived – by way of contrast with all or any process of social conditioning or indoctrination – as conducive to the production of rational, unbiased and tolerant citizens of a liberal-democratic polity' (Carr, 1998a, p.4). Hirst took a stand against both educational traditionalism and progressivism. He argued that traditionalism, understood as limited to the transmission of culture norms, must be replaced with a concern for knowledge itself if education is to be 'based on what is true and not on uncertain opinions and beliefs or temporary values' (Hirst, 1965, p.114). Similarly, Hirst held that progressive advocates of a child-centred cultivation of individual virtue do not 'sufficiently appreciate that these virtues are vacuous unless people are provided with the forms of knowledge and experience to be critical, creative and autonomous with' (Hirst and Peters, 1970, p.31). The logic of Hirst's position was the development of a critical education capable of transcending the inclusive–exclusive divide by enabling pupils to grapple at first hand with the complex issues surrounding spirituality, as outlined above. Such a critical spiritual education would allow pupils to engage intelligently with the ambiguous claims and counter-claims surrounding questions of ultimate truth and meaning.

Successive policy documents issued between 1977 and 1988 retained the *form* of Hirst's focus on a knowledge based curriculum, thus paving the way for the establishment of the National Curriculum in 1988. However, they failed to hold fast to the *substance* of Hirst's proposals, namely, a critical engagement with the search for knowledge. Instead we see emerging in this period a distinction between two educational tasks: the primary educational aim of instilling moral virtue and nurturing a stable and harmonious society, and the secondary educational aim of the attainment of knowledge. For Hirst the two aims were inseparable: it is only by grappling with knowledge that genuine virtue could emerge, only by learning to engage with the ambiguity of spiritual discourse that spiritual development could take place. By 1988 it was clear that, if the form of Hirst's proposals was to be adopted through a subject-based National Curriculum, their underlying philosophical substance was to be set aside. A distinction between knowledge and value was assumed, with knowledge forming the material content of the curriculum, and values constituting the broad aims towards which schools should strive.

Thus in the 1988 Education Reform Act we find spirituality removed from the place originally proposed by HMI, as the subject of informed investigation in the classroom, and located instead as one of the primary aims of education. As we have already noted, pupils were to be taught a balanced and broadly based curriculum in such a way that it 'promotes the spiritual, moral, cultural, mental and physical development of pupils at the school and of society', and 'prepares such pupils for the opportunities, responsibilities and experiences of adult life' (HMSO, 1988, p.1). The implication was clear: spiritual development was to be approached as a pre-established pedagogical target to be worked towards, rather than as part of the material content of the curriculum subject to scrutiny and investigation in the classroom.

The task before teachers was not how to enable pupils to develop appropriate levels of spiritual literacy in a social context marked by high levels of spiritual ambiguity, but rather how to pre-package spirituality in terms of established and obtainable curriculum goals. The critical edge promised by Hirst's proposal is thus effectively replaced by a conservative nurturing of pupil's towards a pre-defined goal which, by necessity, must either be (i) as inclusive as possible, concerned to avoid any hint of controversy, or (ii) committed to a selected exclusive tradition, one capable of imposing a clear spiritual agenda at the expense of silencing alternative voices.

The Consolidation of Spiritual Education

Since the 1988 Education Reform Act there have been a number of significant developments in the sphere of spiritual education, four of which have been of fundamental importance:

1   *Development of an inclusive model of spirituality* – the 1993 discussion paper
     Spiritual and Moral Development, issued by the National Curriculum Council,
     consolidated moves to establish an inclusive definition of spirituality towards
     which schools should strive to lead their pupils (NCC 1993; reissued as SCAA
     1995). It has since become a normative influence on spiritual education.
     Though presented as a discussion paper, it has actually functioned as a provider
     of quasi-authoritative curriculum guidance. It offers a basic, inclusive under-
     standing of spirituality, drawn from HMI's earlier anthropological definition,
     and remains the benchmark against which developments in spiritual education
     are measured. A detailed exploration of the document will be offered in the next
     chapter.

2   *Inspection of spiritual provision in schools* – the importance of spiritual educa-
     tion was reinforced when OFSTED entered the spirituality debate, an
     intervention which reflected government concern that schools were paying insuf-
     ficient attention to social, moral, personal and cultural development (DFE,
     1994). The insistence that a school's provision for spiritual education should be
     the object of OFSTED scrutiny helped ensure that spiritual education avoided
     being reduced to the level of policy rhetoric. So long as inspectors reported on
     the extent to which schools provided opportunities for pupil's spiritual develop-
     ment, so schools would need – however half-heartedly – to attend to the issue.
     However, the intervention of OFSTED also served to galvanise opposition to
     what many progressive educators saw as an increasingly coercive, subject-
     centred and assessment-driven educational system.

3   *Identification of common values* – for traditionalists such progressive resistance
     to educational reforms threatened a return to the relativism of the child-centred
     1960s. The problem, from the traditionalist point of view, was not that values
     were imposed on children, but rather continuing confusion regarding the moral
     and spiritual norms into which children should be nurtured. Increasingly, the
     NCC 'advice' became seen as bland and vacuous as a result of its failure to
     identify concrete spiritual values within a clear spiritual framework. This
     concern led, via the 1996 the SCAA conference 'Education for Adult Life', to
     the establishment of the National Forum for Values in Education and the
     Community. Its mandate was to report on ways of supporting schools in their
     task of contributing to pupil's spiritual and moral development, and to
     'discover whether there are any values upon which there is agreement across
     society' (Talbot and Tate, 1997, p.2). The Forum responded by proposing a set
     of values 'to which, they believed, everyone would subscribe, irrespective of
     their race, ethnic group, religion, age, gender or class', including 'friendship,
     justice, freedom, truth, self-respect and respect for the environment' (ibid.,
     pp.2f.).

4   *Resurgence of spiritual exclusivism* – the work of the Values Forum is best under-
     stood in the light of the educational strategy of the present Labour
     administration, which is clearly concerned to introduce a less ephemeral and
     more specific form of values education in our schools. Indeed, it is perhaps not
     an over-exaggeration to suggest that in recent years the educational pendulum
     has swung away from a concern for inclusivism towards an increasing commit-

ment to exclusive forms of spiritual education. If this is reflected above all in the work of the Values Forum, it also manifests itself in the introduction of Civic Education in schools, and in the current rejuvenation of the Church–State partnership.

Activity

- Draw up a list of the respective strengths and weaknesses of the spiritual education provided in your school.
- What concrete changes would you like to see implemented?

Summary

- A common theme running throughout the historical development of spiritual education has been the ongoing tension between inclusive and exclusive models of spirituality.
- The centrality of spirituality in the 1988 Education Reform Act needs to be interpreted in the light of the collapse of the Christian consensus surrounding spiritual development and the emergence of liberal humanism as the dominant philosophy underlying the public education system.
- The possibility of a spiritual education being taught explicitly as a controversial issue, in which pupils can engage in a critical exploration of conflicting spiritual beliefs and values, though hinted at in the work of Hirst, has not been developed.
- Instead, spirituality has been approached as a general aim towards which schools are expected to direct their pupils.
- This has led to tensions between the established inclusive model of spirituality and recent moves to recover more concrete and exclusive models of spirituality.

7 Inclusive and Exclusive Approaches

The tension between a broad inclusive spirituality acceptable to the many, and a narrow exclusive spirituality acceptable to the few, is a key issue in contemporary spiritual education. Though the general consensus of opinion supports the promotion of an inclusive approach to spiritual pedagogy, there is evidence of the increasing popularity of a range of inclusive models. The tension between these two approaches is the subject of the present chapter.

The dominant inclusive approach to spiritual education is rooted in the struggle for social integration and offers a model of spirituality which seeks to be as open and accommodating as possible. Setting itself against the grain of mainstream opinion this chapter argues that the inclusive model:

- is significantly flawed in its approach to anthropology, history, language, critical thinking and spiritual truth;
- constitutes a distinctive – and hence exclusive – spiritual tradition grounded in a mish-mash of romantic and post-modern ideology;
- effectively silences the voices of alternative 'minority' spiritual traditions.

The alternative policy of selecting from a range of exclusive models – four of which are outlined here – simply makes transparent that which the inclusive model achieves by stealth: the introduction of a strong paternalistic trait, best characterised as benign indoctrination, into the heart of contemporary spiritual education, in a form that pre-packages spirituality and denies pupils the possibility of a critical engagement with its complex and ambiguous reality.

The Struggle for Spiritual Integration

The tensions between inclusive and exclusive approaches to spirituality have helped shape current theory and practice. We have already seen how, in the early 1970s, HMI formulated a distinction between an inclusive anthropological model and an exclusive theological model. Since then the search has been on for an answer to the question posed by Brenda Lealman: 'Can people who approach education from different philosophical/theological viewpoints find a common working definition?'

(Lealman, 1986, p. 67). Lealman's question can be answered in one of three different ways:

- Inclusively – yes – an appropriate common working definition of spirituality can be formulated, and should form the basis of our spiritual pedagogy.
- Exclusively – no – a common working definition cannot be formulated, and consequently spiritual pedagogy must make a strategic choice to select from a range of alternative exclusive models.
- Critically – no – a common working definition is not possible, and as a result spiritual pedagogy must seek to enable pupils to engage critically with a diversity of spiritual traditions.

The general consensus of educational opinion has come out in favour of the first of these options. This response is rooted in the modern experience of spiritual fragmentation, the result, at least in part, of the fact that traditional Christian solutions to the problem of the ultimate meaning and purpose of life have been found wanting. This experience of fragmentation has resulted in an educational commitment to the enhancement of social harmony and stability, rooted in a moral concern for equality of opportunity and drawing on the liberal principles of freedom and tolerance. Above all, inclusivism is driven by a fear of imperialistic power structures, especially as these are embodied in exclusive spiritual traditions.

If these factors explain the rejection of exclusivism as a basis for a common spiritual education, they do not fully explain the speed with which the inclusivist option has been adopted, and the general failure to seriously explore the possibility of an alternative critical path. This is all the more curious given that a strong case can be made that the experience of spiritual fragmentation, coupled with the liberal principles of freedom, tolerance and respect for reason, actually demands a critical pedagogy. There appear to be two major reasons for the eclipse of the critical option in education: (i) the urgent moral need for an education giving priority to social inclusion, linked with fears that such inclusion is undermined by forms of critical education; and (ii) the lack of an established tradition of critical education.

Generally speaking, the assumption that 'to teach something is to advocate it' remains deeply ingrained in our educational theory and practice, and we lack the habit of 'teaching for critical engagement with controversial issues'. A classic example of this is to be found in recent debates concerning the teaching of homosexuality: discussion has focused almost exclusively on the question of what set of values teachers ought to instil in the minds of pupils, rather than with the task of enabling pupils to make informed judgements for themselves, having weighed all sides of the argument.

With these broad considerations in mind, we turn first to a consideration of the composition of the mainstream inclusive model of spirituality.

Activity

Brenda Lealman asks whether people who approach education from different philosophical/theological viewpoints can find a common working definition of spirituality.

- How do you respond to her question?
- What do you consider to be the strengths and weakness of inclusive and exclusive approaches to spiritual pedagogy?

The Inclusive Model

The Priority of Spiritual Experience

The basic structure of the inclusive model of spirituality has been informed by the discussion paper *Spiritual and Moral Development* (SCAA, 1995). It identifies a universal spiritual experience as the foundation and source of our search for life's meaning and purpose. Guided by our feelings and emotions, and our capacity for creativity, such spiritual experience is presented as a fundamental aspect of the human condition, transcending our ordinary everyday experience. It is assumed that we all are capable of a dynamic self-awareness which draws us to the very heart of our existence as human beings, and which is rooted in our search for personal identity and for a sense of the ultimate meaning and purpose of life as we respond to key experiences of death, suffering, evil and beauty. Michael Grimmitt expresses the position adopted by the SCAA document clearly: spirituality is

> a human capacity for a certain type of awareness … the activation of the human capacity for self-transcendence and movement towards a state of consciousness in which the limitations of human finite identity are challenged by the exercise of the creative imagination.
>
> (Grimmitt, 1987, p. 125)

This capacity for spiritual experience resembles, but is not ultimately reducible to, our religious, moral and aesthetic experience. Since such experience is universal it cannot be limited to any specific religious, ethical or artistic tradition, outlook or world-view. Consequently, as Ursula King observes, we can

> look for the spiritual resources within the entire religious heritage of humankind, but we can equally find pointers to spirituality as transcendence and liberation within contemporary secular society.
>
> (King, 1985, p. 137)

The Rejection of Materialism and Rationalism

This affirmation of the significance of spiritual experience goes against the grain of

72

many of the basic assumptions held by modern industrial society. Mircea Eliade is certainly not alone in arguing that modern humanity is fast losing the capacity for spiritual insight, becoming increasingly unable to encounter the sacred in the midst of the profane (1987). The effects of this have plunged society into a state of spiritual crisis. Brian Hill, identifying consumerism as a mark of modernity, suggests that the focus

> on the satisfaction of material needs without sufficient regard to the spiritual nature and needs of human beings ... can lead to people becoming trapped in consumerism, naive about the political forces which manipulate them, and exploitative in human relations.
>
> (Hill, 1989, p. 174)

Such materialism is a direct descendant of the positivist dogma that only verifiable statements about the brute material facts of reality have any claim to truth, and that the language of morality, aesthetics and religion is quite literally meaningless. We are left with a culture in which reason and rationality are prioritised at the expense of feeling and insight, and in which conceptual knowledge is considered to be the only valid form of knowledge.

Advocates of inclusivism argue that we need to protect our capacity for spiritual insight from the threat of materialism by asserting the priority of spiritual experience over rational reflection. 'Spiritual awareness manifests itself first of all in feelings and emotions from which it has to be translated into thought if it is to be talked about at all' (Priestley, 1985, p. 114). King is positive about our ability to achieve this, finding

> clear signs today that the heritage of an empirical and positivist approach to knowledge and experience is faltering and that a new religious sense, atrophied for so long, is being born ... whether in the writings and examples of the saints and mystics of all ages and religions, or in the New Age thinkers and the new physicists today, or in the spiritualities of feminism ... and the peace movement.
>
> (King, 1985, p. 139)

Transcendent Mystery

What is the nature of the reality revealed through such spiritual awareness? Lealman asserts that possession of a spiritually sensitive mind will enable me 'to experience myself within the perspective of transcendence ... and so, to perceive life in a new way, to see the strange within the familiar' (1982, p. 59). But what exactly is it that is 'new', 'transcendent' and 'strange' here?

While *Spiritual and Moral Development* identifies belief as an important dimension of spiritual experience, it is clearly reluctant to engage in any extended conversation about its material content. Advocates of the inclusive model are certainly consistent here, holding that speculation about spiritual dogmas and doctrines can only serve to threaten the authenticity of spiritual experience. Our linguistic constructs are unable to fully grasp the mystery of the universe, since our 'meanings are multi-textured and have many levels of significance ... the focus of language slips forever when it seeks to capture them' (Webster, 1982, p. 87). Consequently we must liberate ourselves from the fruitless search for objective realistic truth and strive instead for 'a new innocence of perception liberated from the cataract of accepted beliefs' (Lealman, 1982, p. 62).

The positive side of this suspicion of doctrine and belief is a celebration of the inherent mystery of life. Spiritual experience 'suggests a mystery, an unseen reality, beyond the life of the individual, pervading the entire world order, with which human persons are invited to enter into relationship and communion' (Slee, 1992, p. 46). Rather than clinging to dogmatic certainties we should learn to rejoice in a universe which is essentially contingent, elusive, and mercurial.

Educating Spiritual Sensibility

What then is the primary task of spiritual education? *Spiritual and Moral Development* presents spirituality as a dimension of education pervading the collective life of the whole school, infiltrating its ethos, Collective Worship and formal curriculum. Here spirituality is to be inculcated and nurtured through the sensitisation of the pupil's curiosity, imagination and intuition.

Since a rational study of spirituality will only serve to destroy the possibility of authentic spiritual experience, the offer of a critical spiritual education never emerges as a genuine option. Instead it is proposed that education concern itself with all those activities which, as Holley puts it, 'sensitise children to the mysteries of life and enable them to view the cosmos, and their place in it, in spiritual terms' (Holley, 1978, p. 65). Authentic spiritual education will seek to sensitise pupils to a heightened awareness of their personal inner space, stimulate their imagination, nurture their creativity and spark their imagination. The ultimate purpose of spiritual education should be to 'give people a greater reliance on the validity of their own inward and private experience' (Priestley, 1992, p. 35).

Activity

Before reading the following section carry out your own critical analysis of the inclusive model of spirituality, paying particular attention to the following:

- its strengths;
- its weaknesses;
- ways in which it might be revised.

Flaws in the Inclusive Model

Spirituality and Anthropology

The inclusive model of spiritual education presents the spiritual quest as an intensely private and personal process, in which we seek spiritual awareness through the contemplation of our subjective 'inner space'. In doing so it relies on an individualistic anthropology rooted in notions of personal autonomy. Charles Taylor has traced the growth of this 'cult of the individual' in western thought, in the process pointing to the possibility of a shift from an 'autonomous' to a 'relational' concept of humanity (Taylor, 1992). Here personal identity is formed not simply through introspection, but equally through our developing relationships with others-in-community, with the natural world, and with the presence – or absence – of God.

Beyond the extremes of a rampant individualism which has brokered the worst excess of free-market capitalism, and an authoritarian collectivism which has under-written communist and fascist totalitarianism, lies the possibility of a communitarianism in which our autonomy is established precisely through our developing relationship with others. Here true freedom is not freedom *from* relationship, but freedom *for* relationship, and our ultimate spiritual values are values shared with those traditions, communities and individuals, who have helped shape us into the people we are.

Spirituality and Tradition

A further criticism of the contemporary consensus is that it lacks any sense of history. It operates with a vision of a random collection of individuals dislocated not only from their communities but also from their historical and cultural roots. Descartes' 'hermeneutic of suspicion', with its rejection of the value and authority of tradition, has been a major contributor to this vision. It has helped popularise the notion that the most effective way to comprehend the world is to put aside our prejudices, suspend the received wisdom of the past, and rely instead on the ideals of neutrality and objectivity.

However, this set of assumptions has not gone uncontested. The importance of tradition becomes clear when one reflects on the dangers of an educational imperialism which would deny pupils from ethnic minorities knowledge of their historical and cultural roots. We cannot avoid our cultural roots, or afford to live out the fiction that we have not been shaped by the various communities into which we were born and which have been responsible for raising us and providing our education. It seems difficult to deny that our spiritual lives are, for good or for ill, shaped by our history, and that this ought to be reflected in any effective form of spiritual education.

Spirituality and Language

Criticism has also been directed against assumptions made by the inclusive model about the role of language in general, and the relationship between language and experience in particular.

Inclusivism operates with a basic understanding of the function of language technically known as 'ostensive definition'. Here the primary role of language is to name objects, whether these be physical objects in the external world or mental 'objects' in the inner realm of our minds. In the latter case, language functions to identify, name and express, however hesitantly and fleetingly, our inner spiritual experiences. Such language is always a secondary expression of primary pre-linguistic experience. If language overreaches itself and attempts to transgress its allotted role, then it falls into the trap of rationalism, in which a complex web of tortuous logical argument serves only to throw a smoke screen over our primal spiritual experience and reinforce a variety of rationalistic ideologies and dogmas.

It has becoming increasingly clear, especially as a result of the later philosophy of Wittgenstein, that this basic model of language as ostensive definition is an inadequate one and that it is necessary to recognise the reality of linguistic diversity and have regard for the social contexts in which language is rooted, and to the various games we play with words. Thus for Ricoeur metaphorical language 'is never purely and simply the symbolism of subjectivity, of the separated human subject, of interiorized self-awareness' (Ricoeur, 1974, p. 309). On the contrary, 'seeking meaning no longer means spelling out consciousness but, rather, deciphering its expressions' (ibid., p. 149).

Recognition of the complexity of language, and of the important connections between language and experience, suggests a spiritual education in which children are taught both to feel *and* to communicate appropriately about their ultimate values and ultimate reality.

Spirituality and Critical Thinking

The distinction between language and experience is not just an academic issue. The inclusivist stress on unreflective experience opens up the possibility of a spiritual emotivism detached from critical reflection, the potential results of which are disturbing. One of the main consequences of a reliance on the authority of our inner experience is the tendency to assume that the stronger the emotion, then the more authentic the experience, and consequently the more justified we are to act upon them. This would, presumably, be fine provided that our inner emotions were always appropriate. But what if our ultimate values are driven by morally unacceptable emotions? What if my untutored feelings lead me into a loathing for those whose racial origins are different to my own?

To put the matter somewhat bluntly, an education that encourages pupils to rely uncritically and unreflectively on their raw emotions runs the risk of nurturing a generation of contented pigs, some of whom may well display anti-social habits and attitudes that are an affront to civilised society. Raw emotion, it seems clear, must be subject to some level of critical scrutiny. Spiritual education ought to seek to produce a generation of discontented philosophers capable of thinking as well as feeling. This is not to place a blind faith in human reason, nor to suggest that our thinking is any less likely to go astray than our raw emotion, but simply to propose that a balanced combination of the two *stands a better chance* of producing appropriate levels of spiritual sensitivity and literacy.

Spirituality and Reality

A final critique of inclusive spirituality picks up the issue of its lack of material content, that is to say, its failure to relate spiritual experience with the reality of how things actually are in the world. In its concern to be acceptable to the widest possible range of opinions the inclusive consensus deliberately avoids specifying the object towards which spiritual experience directs its attention. Instead the teacher is expected to encourage pupils to develop their own personal and idiosyncratic visions of ultimate reality. This raises the vexed question of the relationship between our thought and feelings and the actual order of reality. Does ultimate reality automatically converge with my ultimate concerns? Can my spiritual vision ever be wrong? What is the relationship between ultimate truth and my perceptions of ultimate truth? The failure of the inclusive model to address these questions effectively disenfranchises pupils since it leads to the imposition, by default, of a post-modern solution to these problems, in which the only truth is the truth expressed by the individual pupil. The irony here is that the outward appearance of freedom disguises a subtle yet pervasive indoctrination of pupils into a post-modern world-view.

Having described the inclusive model of spiritual education and drawn attention to a range of specific criticisms levelled at it, it is now possible to draw two broad conclusions from the discussion. First, that it silences and runs roughshod over the self-understanding of a wide range of alternative spiritual traditions, ranging from forms of atheistic humanism through to all the major religious traditions of the world. Second, that despite its concern to offer a universal model acceptable to all, it actually presents a local, parochial and hence exclusive model of spirituality, rooted in a mishmash of romanticism and post-modernism.

Activity

- Review your own critique of the inclusive model in the light of the various arguments presented in this section.
- Has the inclusive approach been effectively undermined?
- Are there any counter-arguments that can be put forward in its defence?

Four Exclusive Alternatives

The dominant inclusive model of spirituality has been seen be to fundamentally flawed: (i) it operates with an uncritical model of education; (ii) its core assumptions regarding anthropology, tradition, language, critical thinking and truth are the subject of fundamental criticism; (iii) it fails to do justice to the self-understanding of a wide range of alternative spiritual traditions; and (iv) it constitutes an exclusive spiritual tradition that is a product of post-Enlightenment Western thought.

It is not, then, surprising to encounter the emergence of attempts to replace this rather bland inclusivism with a range of exclusive traditions keen both to affirm and justify far more robust accounts of spiritual truth. There is space here to do no more than glance briefly at four case-studies.

Adrian Thatcher: Christian Orthodoxy

Thatcher's advocacy of an orthodox Trinitarian Christian foundation for spiritual education proceeds on the basis of his definition of spirituality as 'the practice of the human love of God and neighbour' (Thatcher, 1996, p. 119). His stance is a radical one, which cannot simply be reduced to the level of a conservative transmission of traditional national values coated in a pseudo-Christian veneer. Thatcher is sharply opposed to the work of the Values Forum, rejecting its ahistorical rootless base, questioning the dubious assumption that it has achieved public consensus, and above all challenging 'its calm banishment of God in the name of a humanistic morality' (Thatcher, 1999a, p. 5). He argues that the problems of operating within a Christian theological framework are no more difficult than those encountered by the liberal consensus seekers, since both operate within world-views that lay claim to universality. It is not clear as to the extent to which Thatcher wishes to see Christian spirituality provide the basis of spiritual education in state schools, but he is clear that it must form the foundation of spiritual pedagogy in Christian educational institutions.

David Hay: Religious Universalism

We have already had occasion to explore David Hay's work in some detail in Chapter 2, noting his belief that empirical research provides scientific grounds to affirm belief in an objective, transcendent divine reality. We have, he writes, 'grounds for some confidence in the objective reality of the states of awareness achieved in contemplative practice, whatever the variety of interpretations provided by the different traditions' (Hay, 1982, p. 49). Hay goes on to affirm that such experience of transcendent reality is a universal feature of human experience, and as such demands a universal theology in which the broad range of religious and spiritual traditions promise to become vehicles for the stimulation of such experience. Just as other subjects in the curriculum are rooted in human experience, so spiritual education should be grounded in the universal experience of objective transcendent reality. However, the legacy of materialism and rationalism, coupled with the excesses of techno-science, and rampant consumerism, have produced a spirit of suspicion towards such experience. Consequently, public spiritual education just assumes a subversive and radical form, seeking to challenge the misplaced assumptions of modernity by stimulating children's capacity for spiritual experience as a means of challenging the cultural norms of contemporary Western culture.

Mike Newby: Secular Humanism

Newby advocates a secular humanistic spirituality that seeks the development of a specifically non-religious spirituality (Newby, 1994, 1996). It is to be concerned with the discernment of good and evil, the journey towards meaning and purpose, and the liberal search for human well being. This humanistic spiritual journey must be sharply differentiated from a spirituality grounded in the supernatural realism of orthodox theology. There is, he claims, 'a shared spirituality abroad in our secular culture ... in which traditional religious belief is superficial or local, and often both' (Newby, 1994, p. 17). Newby goes on to argue that 'this secular spirituality must not be seen as a rich land to be reclaimed by the church' (ibid.). Instead it must be appropriated on its own terms, as a 'post-religious spirituality of agapaistic love rising out of the ashes of dead orthodoxy' (ibid.). He attributes an 'overriding authority [to] our shared framework of secular value commitments' (ibid., p. 19), and goes on to suggest that schooling may only be 'deemed educationally successful insofar as it advances spiritual development through secular traditions of knowledge and understanding' (ibid.).

Clive Erricker: Post-modern Relativism

Erricker adopts a self-consciously post-modern stance, arguing that 'through metaphor we generate meaning and order reality for ourselves in pursuit of mental and spiritual health' (Erricker, 1993, p. 138). Such language, he suggests, constitutes a reality created by inter-subjective communication. 'It is not a matter of distinguishing between religious and non-religious world views nor of determining the ultimate worth of any metaphorical reality but arriving at an appreciation of the metaphorical realities that we all hold' (ibid., p. 144). Here, in an anti-realistic move typical of post-modernism, language becomes the ultimate reality: the question of whether it is capable of depicting an objective world is subservient to the instrumental issue of 'how far ... particular metaphors contribute to or detract from our well-being' (ibid., p. 138). Erricker refers to the iconic quality of mind, the mental imaging that enables us to construct the stories by which we live: 'metaphor actually generates meaning ... it constructs a landscape in which we have a place' (ibid., p. 139). Spiritual education should have no concern with objective reality, merely with the pragmatic activity of communicating a rich diversity of metaphorical images. 'Developing communication between and reflecting upon the plurality of our metaphorical perceptions is one of the primary educational tasks that we must address' (ibid., p. 138). Through such an exchange of vision individuals may create for themselves metaphorical realities that contribute to their physical, mental and spiritual health. 'Learning starts by avoiding the objectification of children and the mythologies of others that we introduce them to ... what we are concerned with here is ... helping children to construct their own enabling metaphors' (ibid., p. 146).

Activity

Note down your critical response to each of these exclusive models.

- Do any of them constitute coherent world-views?
- Are any of them able to presenting a viable vision of the ultimate meaning and purpose of life?
- Ought any of them be allowed to form the foundation of a public programme of spiritual education?

Each of these four representative exclusive models faces similar problems: if they are to be introduced into mainstream education with any level of integrity then two conditions must apply. First, they must actually be true, since the imposition of an exclusive tradition that is not true is simply unacceptable on both moral and intellectual grounds. Second, and equally significantly, they must not only be true, but must also be *seen to be true*, if they are to stand any chance of establishing their legitimacy in the eyes of teachers, parents, pupils and wider society. It is certainly possible that any of the four examples presented above may indeed actually present accurate accounts of ultimate reality, and hence offer appropriate spiritual accounts of the ultimate meaning and purpose of life. The problem is that, at present at least, there is no universal standard against which such truth claims may be judged; consequently there is no public consensus regarding the veracity of any of the four models.

It is simply not good enough to claim that Christianity, or religious universalism, or secular atheism or post-modern relativism represent deep-rooted, informed and properly thought-out spiritual traditions. Erricker's observation that spiritual relativism 'is a recognised philosophical standpoint that affirms divergence of view and on this basis calls for a consensus of values whilst accepting the distinctiveness of different epistemological and faith stances' misses the point that its philosophical foundations are simply incompatible with, and unacceptable to, alternative spiritual traditions (Erricker, 2000, p. 190). Unless a spiritual tradition can demonstrate wide-ranging public acceptance, its imposition in the sphere of public education will be perceived as an aggressive and unacceptable act of (attempted) indoctrination.

Spiritual education thus finds itself caught on the horns of a dilemma, forced to choose between inclusive blandness, or exclusive authoritarianism. At the end of the day neither option escapes the charge of educational paternalism, since both paths stand accused of attempting to mould children into a preconceived spiritual framework. While this reality has always been transparent for the range of exclusive models, the argument of this chapter suggests it ought now to be viewed as being equally transparent in the case of the inclusive model, since it is clearly in possession of its own world-view, prior commitments and bedrock assumptions.

The result of all this is that, so long as we retain an uncritical model of education, battle for control over the right to transmit any spiritual tradition will be a political issue, in which a fight for power in the educational arena equates with the fight for the right of the victor to impose one particular spiritual tradition on children. Yet, as Plato pointed about centuries ago in *Book One* of *The Republic*, 'might is right' is an unacceptable position on intellectual, moral and educational grounds (Plato, 1963, pp. 576ff.).

Summary

- The chapter described how the inclusive model of spiritual education gives priority of spiritual experience, rejects materialistic rationalism, celebrates mystery and advocates the cultivation of spiritual sensibility.
- Four basic flaws in the inclusive model were identified: (i) it operates with a limited nurturing model of education; (ii) its core assumptions about anthropology, tradition, language, critical thinking and truth are not the subject of universal assent; (iii) it fails to do justice to the self-understanding of a wide range of alternative spiritual traditions; and (iv) it constitutes an exclusive spiritual tradition that is a product of late twentieth-century Western thought.
- The various exclusive models of spirituality – of which four were presented as brief case studies – simply make explicit that which is implicit in the inclusive model: the fact that contemporary spiritual education proceeds by attempting to resolve the problems associated with spirituality prior to the learning process, rather than allowing pupils to engage critically with the issues for themselves.

8 Beyond the Inclusive/Exclusive Impasse?

The previous chapter showed how spiritual education tends to oscillate between two extremes: on the one hand an inclusivism that, designed to win approval across a broad range of spiritual opinions, tends towards a vacuous relativism; on the other a range of exclusive models which, concerned to provide spiritual education with a material content, threaten to indoctrinate pupils into specific world-views. The present chapter seeks to discover a path beyond this inclusive–exclusive impasse, arguing that curriculum development need not be reduced to a straight choice between the two. There is no reason why spiritual pedagogy should not be reconceptualised in a form that transcends what is, at the end of the day, a particularly restrictive vision of education. One possible route forward, already hinted at above, is through the development of a critical model of spiritual education capable of equipping children with the wisdom, insight and skills necessary for them to find their own way through the difficult terrain of spirituality. This is a significantly different enterprise from a post-modern spiritual pedagogy in which pupils are encouraged to follow their desires and instincts, since a critical pedagogy will demand from them appropriate levels of spiritual literacy.

This chapter focuses on the work of John Hull and is designed to provide a bridge between the inclusive/exclusive impasse and the presentation of a critical spiritual pedagogy that follows in Part III. It begins by sketching an overview of Hull's liberal approach to spiritual education, suggesting that it embraces a critical dimension that points beyond the inclusive–exclusive divide. However, closer analysis reveals a tendency to close down discussion of controversial issues prematurely: driven by his concern to protect the liberal values of freedom and tolerance, Hull does not allow his programme to develop a sufficiently critical edge. Despite this Hull's work brings us face to face with the programme of critical spiritual education proposed in Part III.

John Hull: Spiritual Solidarity

John Hull, Professor of Religious Education at the University of Birmingham, was one of the chief architects of the anti-dogmatic multi-faith Religious Education that is now the established norm in the vast majority of our schools. Hull's programme of spiritual education is grounded in his advocacy of the dignity, freedom and mutual solidarity of all children, regardless of race, culture and creed. Observing that Article 14:1 of the United Nations Convention on the Rights of the Child affirms the right of pupils to freedom of thought, conscience and religion, Hull advocates a schooling that 'educates the conscience of the child and develops the child's powers of free thought' (Hull, 1998, p. 59). Pupils 'are not to become mere objects of instruction but are to be developed as expressive and creative agents' (ibid., p. 60).

This strategy of focusing on the child's freedom of thought rather than the material content of the curriculum enables Hull to introduce a critical dimension into his educational thinking. His primary concern is not with the identification of a pre-packaged model of spirituality, whether inclusive or exclusive, but the empowerment of pupils to think for themselves. If genuine freedom of thought, expression and creativity is to flourish, then education must concern itself with three specific issues:

- the pluralistic and multi-cultural character of British society;
- the specific culture from which the child originates;
- the values of civilisations which are 'different'.

(ibid, pp. 60f.)

Hull contends that these perspectives 'are essential if the role of education is to be fulfilled in enabling children to develop freedom of thought, and to explore their cultural and spiritual heritage' (ibid., p. 61).

This leads Hull to define what he calls the 'ingredients of spirituality' in terms of a cluster of moral virtues rather than any specific religious or secular world-view. He quotes with approval from the preamble of the *United Nations Convention*: 'the child should be fully prepared to live an individual life in society and brought up ... in the spirit of peace, dignity, tolerance, freedom, equality and solidarity' (ibid.). Such a virtue-based perspective refuses to reduce spirituality to the mere cultivation of introspective awareness, and points instead to a relational model of spiritual identity. Hull is clear that 'spirituality exists not inside people but between them' (ibid., p. 66). It follows that spiritual education must concern itself with the cultivation of solidarity and communion in a pluralistic society. 'Spiritual education inspires young people to live for others ... [and] seeks to recreate community through participation in the lives of others' (ibid.).

Hull's approach takes us a significant step beyond the models explored in the previous chapter:

- *beyond inclusivism* – there is no place for a vacuous inclusive spirituality devoted to an unstructured, emotive and relativistic exploration of inner space;
- *beyond exclusivism* – nor is there a place for the uncritical imposition of a specific spiritual tradition, whether that be Thatcher's Christianity, Hay's universalism, Newby's atheism or Erricker's post-modernism;
- *towards critical solidarity* – there must, however, be both time and space for a spiritual education concerned with the cultivation of the critical freedom of pupils to engage in a spiritual search driven by the values of peace, dignity, tolerance, freedom, equality and solidarity.

Activity

Hull suggests that pupils 'are not to become mere objects of instruction but are to be developed as expressive and creative agents'.

- What are the implications of this for spiritual education?

The Dangers of Religionism

Hull is constantly aware of the dangers inherent in the shift from a content to a process-driven curriculum. The freedom of the child from the imposition of any specific spiritual tradition – whether inclusive or exclusive – runs the risk of creating a vacuum in which they become vulnerable to abusive power structures and ideological manipulation. Unconstrained freedom runs the risk of forcing children out of the paternalistic frying pan into an anarchic fire, and consequently the practice of freedom must be carefully cultivated if it is not to lead to abuse. It is here, however, in its opposition to cultural and political forces which threaten to undermine his spirituality of mutual solidarity, that Hull's proposal comes unstuck.

Hull offers a concrete example of the potential dangers of allowing children unconstrained freedom to encounter alternative social and cultural values. The *Song of Roland* is the product of a medieval tradition set, at least in is final form, in the time of the Crusades and which presents the hero Roland as the 'symbol of Christian heroism struggling against Islam' (Hull. 1998, p. 54). Hull shows how an abridgement and adaptation of the medieval text intended for use in schools presents a hostile, distorted and highly prejudicial view of Islam. The text seriously misrepresents Islamic theology, as for example in the accusation that Muslims 'made an idol of the prophet Mahomet and worshipped him along with other heathen gods' (ibid.). The abuse of Islam in the text of the book is exacerbated 'by pictures in which handsome red cross knights are shown in battle with evil-looking foreigners, wearing turbans and slippers with pointed tips' (ibid., p. 55).

Books such as these reflect attitudes for which Hull coins the term 'religionism', and it is worth quoting his definition at length:

> Religionism describes an adherence to a particular religion which involves the identity of the adherent so as to support tribalistic or nationalistic solidarity. The identity which is fostered by religionism depends upon rejection and exclusion. We are better than they are. We are orthodox; they are infidel. We are believers; they are unbelievers. We are right; they are wrong. The other is identified as the pagan, the heathen, the alien, the stranger, the invader, the one who threatens us and our way of life. Religion is in principle universal in its outlook but religionism is committed to the partial.
>
> (ibid., p. 56)

In the face of the pervasive power of religionism the mere cultivation of children's freedom is not enough. Hull argues that the spiritual virtues will only be able to flourish in the face of religionist assaults if education accepts the responsibility for anti-religionist training. Mere tolerance does not go far enough: religionist attitudes must be identified, isolated, and deconstructed. 'Just as special educational techniques exist in order to combat racism, so we need a special educational programme to combat religionism' (ibid.).

Hull here implicitly invokes the liberal 'paradox of tolerance'. As unpacked by Karl Popper, the paradox affirms the principle that the one thing tolerance must *not* tolerate is intolerance itself: 'it may easily turn out that they (the intolerant) are not willing to meet us on the level of rational argument ... we should therefore claim, in the name of tolerance, the right not to tolerate the intolerant' (Popper, 1966, p. 265). Hull is not advocating an unconstrained freedom for children, but a freedom dependent on the prudent cultivation of their ability to resist the forces of intolerance.

Such anti-religionism can, of course, operate within a critical framework, providing pupils with the skills and insights to identify and challenge religionism for themselves. However, Hull recognises a point at which opposition to religionism cannot be left in the hands of pupils; at this stage censorship becomes necessary for their own protection. Of the adapted version of the *Song of Roland* he writes: 'In view of the Gulf War and the ancient resentments which it has aroused, it is most unfortunate that a work of this kind is still to be found on the shelves of school libraries' (Hull, 1998, p. 55). Every school library, he continues, needs an equal opportunities policy, and school librarians must be critically vigilant towards their resources and willing to remove religionist literature from library shelves.

In the case of classic works of literature which are inherently religionist or racist Hull suggests turning to modern abridgements which avoid projecting present cultural tensions back into the past. At the same time he acknowledges the dangers inherent in a rewriting of history that produces an idealised non-religionist past. 'There is a limit to which one can introduce expurgated versions of these classics without fundamentally changing their message' (ibid., p. 57). In such cases it may be possible to use a religionist book provided children have their attention drawn to its nature and a critical reading of the text is encouraged. Here Hull's strategy shifts from a negative education which seeks to protect children from harmful contact with religionism to a positive education which encouraged a critical encounter with sectarian attitudes. Is the demon of religionism best defeated by locking it up out of harm's way, or through a straight fight to the finish?

Hull shows a clear preference for a negative education which protects children from contamination by religionism. In doing so he fails to develop sufficiently the positive value of actively engaging in a critical manner with religionist texts, and of using such encounters as a means of throwing light on the nature of sectarianism and therefore deepening children's critical awareness and understanding. In the case of the *Song of Roland*, for example, the fact that Roland's enemies in early versions of the tradition were not Muslims but Basques, and that the demonisation of Islam that later develops in the tradition represents a revision of what was originally a very different sectarian story, presents an ideal opportunity to encourage children to explore some of the ways in which religionism operates through a concrete case study.

Activity

The line between a negative education concerned to protect children from morally unacceptable material, and a positive education that encourages pupils to grapple with the material for themselves, is traditionally a particularly difficult one to draw.

- List the pros and cons of both negative and positive education.
- Produce a set of guidelines for classroom teachers designed to help them to clarify their thinking and decision making in this area.
- What difference should the respective ages of the children and young people being taught make?
- Should the guidelines change as pupils progress through the various Key Stages?

'Give me a fish and I eat for a day; teach me to fish and I eat for the rest of my life'. This ancient Chinese proverb illuminates the differences between the respective positions of Hull and advocates of critical spiritual education. Hide the demon of religionism from pupils and they enjoy the immediate experience of spiritual solidarity but without any adequate preparation for encounters with religionist attitudes outside of the classroom. Teach children how to critically engage with religionism in the relative security of the classroom situation and the possibility opens up of providing skills of moral and spiritual discernment they can use for the rest of their lives. The difference here, it is important to stress, is one of degree rather than an either/or choice: the suggestion here is that the primary educational instinct of the teacher ought to be a carefully orchestrated critical engagement rather than censorial protection.

Hull's Implicit Paternalism

It has been argued that Hull is a little too quick to sweep religionism under the carpet in order to protect children from contamination, and a little too slow to allow children a critical encounter with forms of religionism as a means of enhancing their critical grasp of the issues. The paternalistic instinct we observed in the previous two chapters is thus present, though to a significantly lesser degree, in Hull's proposals. This becomes clear when we look at Hull's interpretation of the prevalence of religionism within established religious traditions. Here his concern to advocate the virtue of spiritual solidarity leads him into a significant and unacceptable misrepresentation of religion.

Hull argues that 'it seems difficult for religions to evolve without taking on religionist tendencies', and mentions specifically Christian attitudes towards Judaism in the New Testament, Islamic attitudes towards both Christianity and Judaism and Protestantism in its initial struggle with Catholicism (1998. p. 56). In all three cases Hull holds that the need to confirm and protect sectarian identity cultivates religionist attitudes.

Hull identifies similar sectarian attitudes at work among those conservative Christians, religious educators and politicians who favour a form of Religious Education in which the distinctiveness and separateness of individual religious traditions in general, and Christianity in particular, are affirmed. Hull's own preference is for a thematic approach to religious teaching which identifies the inter-connection between different religious traditions and stresses their mutuality and common links. This thematic approach, Hull's opponents fear, will lead to a multi-faith mishmash in which the distinctiveness of individual religious traditions are dissolved in a universal theological stew. Hull takes issue with this critics here:

> The horror of mish-mash is the horror of a threatened identity ... The expression 'mish-mash' and other similar metaphors of disgusting food mixtures used by Christian religionists ... spring from a desire for an elitist social and cognitive purity.
>
> (ibid., pp. 111, 117)

Hull believes that the presentation in the classroom of individual religious traditions as distinctive entities, in which clear lines of demarcation are drawn between one faith and another, serves three purposes:

- *it undermines the universal nature of religion* – Hull identifies authentic religious traditions in terms of their inclusivity and universalism, as opposed to religionist distortions which emphasise exclusivity and parochialism. 'Religion is in principle universal in its outlook but religionism is committed to the partial' (ibid., p. 56);
- *it undermines the possibility of interfaith dialogue* – for the religionist 'there must be no mutuality, no sharing of the ideals and hopes of the other, no dialogue' (ibid., p. 115);
- *it undermines a liberal communitarian spirituality* – by drawing lines of division rather than connection it fails to equip children with the liberal virtues of tolerance and understanding, and plays no part in 'in widening identity from the tribe and from the nation to all that is truly human' (ibid., p. 117).

There is an assumption here that the primary core of all the major religious traditions is universal rather than particular, inclusive rather than exclusive, and that religionist and sectarian tendencies are the result of secondary attempts to preserve the identity and purity of specific faith traditions. The problem with this is that it leaves almost all the major religious traditions of the world branded as 'religionist'. The distinctive world-views and truth claims of Buddhism, Christianity, Islam, Judaism, Sikhism, etc. are simply not compatible with Hull's depiction of universal religion. As we have already had occasion to observe, when orthodox Christianity proclaims Jesus of Nazareth as God incarnate they are affirming a belief that stands in flat contradiction with Islamic belief in Jesus as a prophet of Allah. There is here a significant failure to attend openly and honestly to the voices of specific religious traditions, to recognise and identify genuine difference, and to offer minority traditions appropriate acknowledgement and respect. Simply because the exclusive truth claims of specific religious traditions fail to conform to a liberal universal theology is not sufficient justification for the imposition of what, in extreme cases, can be tantamount to an act of cultural imperialism.

It is important to note also that an exclusive truth claim does not automatically coincide with religionism. Muslim respect for Christians and Jews as fellow 'people of the book' is grounded in an honest acceptance of difference rather than an imposition of a universally acceptable theological framework. Similarly, recent developments in Roman Catholic understanding to the relationship of the church with other world faiths is eirenic and respectful in tone, apologetic and contrite in the face of its (frequently) religionist past, and accommodating in its content, all achieved without the need to compromise Christian exclusivism. The connection Hull draws between exclusivist theology and religionist practice is, at the very least, a matter of dispute. It follows that he is a little too quick to draw lines between religionist and non-religionist manifestations of religion, a little over-hasty in adjudicating between what constitutes an original authentic religious tradition and what constitutes a secondary religionist distortion

A further significant omission in Hull's argument is a failure to acknowledge the diversity of possible approaches to interfaith dialogue. Alongside his advocacy of dialogue grounded in the recognition of common humanity communicating within a universal theological framework stands the possibility of dialogue grounded in a mutual acceptance of difference, and a mutual agreement to pursue conversation despite fundamental contradictions between belief systems. Hull makes reference to the problems of political sectarianism, suggesting that education should be judged on whether it 'takes us nearer to the separated communities of Belfast and Beirut or nearer to the life of love' (1998, p. 116). One clear lesson of the peace processes in both Northern Ireland and the Middle East has been that effective dialogue demands not the fiction of false accommodation but a mutual recognition of difference. The notion of tolerance carries with it the implication of acceptance of, and respect for, difference: if everything is dissolved into a common humanitarian melting pot then difference is eradicated and tolerance becomes a redundant term.

Hull thus finds himself faced with the dilemma of needing to misrepresent the self-understanding of significant bodies of religious opinion in order to implement his anti-religionist programme. The critical openness promised by Hull's shift from a concern for the material content of spirituality to an understanding of spirituality as communal relationship is thus not completely fulfilled. A strong, if only implicit, paternalism runs throughout his whole programme. Consequently he misses the opportunity to establish a communitarian spiritual education that proceeds not only by identifying common ground but also by recognising points of tension and conflict.

Activity

> Humankind cannot bear very much reality.
>
> (T.S. Eliot, 'Burnt Norton', 1974, p. 190)

- Spend a few moments reflecting on Eliot's words, then brainstorm your responses to them.
- What light do they shed on the discussion presented in this chapter?
- How far should spiritual education go in exploring the depths of human spirituality, both in its healthy and pathological manifestations?
- Should schools impose any practical, moral, intellectual or spiritual limits to such exploration? Why? What? How?

There is much to be said against a rose-tinted idealisation of spiritual solidarity, and even more to be said in favour of the spiritual virtues being realistically rooted in the actual tensions and contradictions that are part and parcel of our pluralistic culture. The reality of difference, and the ways in which we learn to respond appropriately to such difference, are fundamentally important in the development of authentic spirituality. Such issues need to be actively and openly engaged with in the classroom if spiritual education is not to slip back into paternalism. The possibility of just such a critical spiritual education is the subject of Part III.

Summary

- By shifting attention from the material content of spirituality to the notion of the virtue of spiritual solidarity Hull promises to open up the possibility a critical spiritual education that transcends educational paternalism.
- The threat of sectarian religionism, however, leads Hull to stress the importance of protecting children from potential contamination by a range of socially unacceptable spiritual attitudes and opinions.
- This leads Hull to advocate an idealistic model of spiritual development that fails to take full account of the significance of conflict and tension as an educational resource upon which a genuinely critical spiritual education might be grounded.

Part III

Towards a Critical Spiritual Education

9 Principles of Critical Spiritual Education

Part I described how the spiritual quest for life's ultimate meaning and purpose has fragmented into a complex network of beliefs, attitudes and opinions. Part II suggested that contemporary spiritual education, oscillating as it does between a vacuous inclusivism and a dogmatic exclusivism, has been unable to produce adequate levels of spiritual literacy. Currently many of our pupils are denied the opportunity to cultivate the wisdom necessary to respond intelligently to the maze of spiritual possibilities facing them at the dawn of the third millennium. At the heart of this book stands the thesis that the dilemma of current spiritual education lies in its failure to engage critically with the ambiguity of spirituality.

Part III sets out positive proposals for a critical spiritual education. It does so in the belief that an effective spiritual pedagogy is possible provided spirituality is treated as a controversial issue demanding the implementation of teaching and learning strategies which enable pupils to wrestle directly with the equivocal nature of spirituality.

The proposal of such a critical spiritual pedagogy is presented in four stages: Chapter 9 establishes five basic principles for critical spiritual education; Chapter 10 proposes a revised agenda; Chapter 11 suggests that spiritual education needs to be rooted in an effective policy of spiritual nurture; Chapter 12 argues that spiritual nurture must to be supplemented by a process of critical emancipation.

The present chapter aims to establish five basic principles for a critical spiritual pedagogy. Effective teaching for spiritual literacy must do the following:

- extricate itself from the current malaise of spiritual education;
- transcend the intrinsic–extrinsic impasse;
- develop a critical awareness of ideology;
- assimilate liberalism as an interim ethic rather than as a closed world-view;
- replace educational foundationalism with a process-oriented pedagogy.

Beyond the Malaise of Contemporary Spiritual Education

Despite the significant growth of spiritual education since 1988 the fact remains that an effective nation-wide programme of spiritual pedagogy has yet to be implemented. Spirituality remains something of a Cinderella subject in the classroom:

pockets of excellent innovative practice constantly find themselves smothered by a widespread mixture of blandness and apathy. The general malaise retards the possibility of the emergence of a critical spiritual pedagogy. A number of factors are at work here.

Lack of Appropriate Training

It is difficult to ignore widespread concerns regarding professional competency. Many teachers, despite being effective teachers of their specialist subjects, actively avoid the task of spiritual education, not because they view the issues as being inappropriate for classroom investigation, but because they feel they lack the training, insight, knowledge and skills necessary for them to do a professional job. This is especially so in the light of the inherently ambiguous nature of spirituality in modern society, and the increasingly technical and specialist nature of the processes through which spirituality is investigated in the academy.

Absence of Good Practice

The situation is not helped by the frequent absence of examples of good practice on which teachers can draw. All too often hesitant and half-hearted attempts on the part of senior management to establish a policy for spiritual education are coupled with a lack of effective implementation in the classroom.

Fear of Extremism

There certainly appears to be a residual fear in many schools that the agenda of spiritual education has been hijacked by the 'extremist' forces of either reactionary Christianity or New Age activism. Such suspicion can lead to a failure to engage with questions of ultimate truth in the classroom on the grounds that such issues ought to be confined to the realm of private belief. If such resistance effectively silences the voices of spiritual 'extremism', it does so only at the cost of stifling educational debate.

Innate Conservatism

The lack of a critical foundation for spiritual education is further exacerbated by an establishment concerned more with papering over the cracks of a divided society than with the cultivation of spiritual literacy. However benign and well meaning, these conservative forces undermine the integrity of spiritual education by insisting that it be grounded in an idealistic ethic of spiritual harmony rather than in a realistic and educative engagement with the reality of spiritual discord.

Avoidance of Spiritual Ambiguity

The spiritual quest for the ultimate meaning and purpose of life is as vital for civilisation at the dawn of the third millennium as at any previous point in human history. The ambiguity of the current spiritual situation underlines the urgent need for effective education in this area. The core educational challenge is to grasp the nettle and acknowledge that the issue of ultimate truth is a controversial one, about which there is no public consensus. Despite this, current theory and practice continue to view this situation as a problem rather than as an opportunity.

Absence of good practice and concerns about professional competency are not, at the end of the day, issues of long-term significance. In suggesting this, I do not wish to downgrade the very real concerns of individual teachers: in such a fledgling area of curriculum development one would be surprised *not* to encounter these problems, and they are already beginning to be addressed in PGCE courses and INSET programmes. The most serious issue facing spiritual education in the long term is the lack of any sustained vision of how to introduce a critical edge into the heart of spiritual pedagogy. This situation is rooted in a fear of extremism, an innately conservative establishment and an instinct to bypass the controversial nature of spirituality. The urgent need for spiritual education to extricate itself from the current malaise of spiritual education is, then, the first of the five principles of critical spiritual education identified in this chapter.

Activity

It has been suggested that the following factors are largely responsible for the current malaise of spiritual education:

  (i) lack of training;
 (ii) absence of good practice;
(iii) fear of extremism;
(iv) a conservative establishment;
 (v) avoidance of spiritual ambiguity.

- Is the suggestion that contemporary spiritual education is moribund justifiable?
- Are there other factors that ought to be added to this list?
- Rank the factors in order of significance for your school.
- Suggest ways in which they might be challenged and overcome.

Beyond the Intrinsic–Extrinsic Impasse

The contemporary consensus surrounding spiritual education, as outlined in Chapter 7, is committed to an intrinsic model of spirituality that seeks to embrace a universal perspective and win acceptance from the widest possible range of traditions and world-views. This attempt to identify a common generic understanding of spirituality has been a key dimension of national educational strategy since the 1988

Education Reform Act. The increasing centralisation of educational policy in recent years, a process inextricably linked with the consolidation of the National Curriculum, has served to reinforce the perceived need for a common approach.

As has already been noted, a frequent criticism of the intrinsic approach is its advocacy of an abstract spirituality marked by four key factors:

- dislocation from any specific social, cultural, and historical tradition;
- preference for pre-linguistic and ahistorical spiritual experience;
- lack of material content;
- rejection of the option of critical reflection.

David Carr has proposed a path beyond the impasse of the inclusive approach to spiritual education. He acknowledges that, in the absence of any shared spiritual vision, 'it may be more natural to many people in the secular contexts of modernity to speak of different and diverse qualities of spiritual *experience* or *feeling* than of traditions of spiritual truth, knowledge and virtue' (Carr, 1996, p. 160). However, such abstract feeling does little to enable children to engage intelligently with the spiritual debate. Carr argues that an education that cultivates emotive reliance on inner experience and parades before children 'disinherited and disjointed fragments of the life of different and diverse human cultures' cannot possibly provide children with any substantial spiritual nourishment (ibid., p. 173). Such a reductionist spirituality is 'inclined to explain the spiritual in terms which are independent of the substantial metaphysical, ontological and epistemological commitments evidently presupposed by traditional conceptions of spiritual development' (ibid., p. 163).

Carr is adamant that if spiritual education is to retain any level of integrity it must ditch the intrinsic approach and opt instead for a spiritual education rooted in a specific spiritual tradition. 'No genuine understanding of spirituality can really be available short of a substantial examination of (even initiation into) the reflection, practices and achievements of some actual spiritual tradition or other' (ibid., p. 173). Carr is surely correct: if spiritual education is to have any chance of being effective it must engage with concrete spiritual traditions rather than with an inclusive hybrid.

However, the danger inherent in Carr's proposal is that it will result in an educational sectarianism in which a school, having embraced a specific spiritual tradition, effectively isolates itself from a range of alternative spiritual traditions. Carr proposes a leap from the inclusive frying pan into the exclusive fire and as a result does not offer a viable path beyond the inclusive–exclusive impasse. If the current inclusive consensus promises pseudo-unity at the expense of diversity, then Carr's critique of inclusivism – despite scoring a direct hit on its target – promises no more than sectarian diversity at the expense of unity. What is needed is a pedagogy capable of addressing both the universality of humanity's spiritual aspirations and the actuality of distinct spiritual traditions. This will involve neither common consensus nor sectarian fragmentation, but rather mutual recognition and dialogue between diverse traditions. The concerns of the many and of the few, of society as a whole and of the specific traditions that make up society, are not mutually exclusive. This need to transcend the intrinsic–extrinsic impasse by doing justice both to the integrity of specific spiritual traditions and to the value of communication between divergent traditions is the second of the five principles of critical spiritual education identified in this chapter.

Activity

- How might education combine a recognition of the universality of our spiritual aspirations with a commitment to the integrity of specific spiritual traditions?
- What shared interests, questions and concerns might inform conversation between humanistic, liberal and post-modern spiritual traditions without compromising their distinct identities?

Ideological Representation and Critical Thinking

From a Marxist perspective the concept of ideology carries with it a pejorative connotation: the ideological function of spiritual education is to bolster the infrastructure of society by protecting the self-interest of those in positions of power. For a Marxist ideology is something that must be overcome. However, the post-modern criticism of the liberal myth of neutrality – the misplaced belief that it is possible to establish an objective value-free perspective on reality – has made it clear that all discourse is inevitability ideological. It follows that the proper task of critical education is not to attempt to overcome ideology, but to develop in pupils a critical awareness of the ideological power structures that are simply part and parcel of ordinary life.

The problems presented by the inclusive model of spirituality are compounded by the fact that many of its supporters remain ignorant of its ideological nature, oblivious of its parochial roots and naïve in their assumption that it enjoys universal cross-cultural validity. There is a disconcerting lack of self-criticism in the deliberations of some spiritual educators at this point. What is urgently required is a new dimension of critical reflection directed towards the educational discourse of spirituality itself. It can be argued that the spiritual educator is 'under an obligation to expose for examination the fundamental axioms, the prior decisions about what is allowed to count as evidence, which underlie his (*sic.*) way of understanding' (Newbigin, 1982, p. 99).

What is needed is a critical hermeneutic capable of penetrating beyond the surface appearance of any given spiritual representation and exposing its fundamental commitments, presuppositions and ideological roots. Effective curriculum development must enable both teachers and pupils to learn how to expose manipulative ideologies and identify the forces of power and domination operating within spiritual discourse.

Activity

- Carry out a critical analysis of (i) your own personal spiritual tradition, and (ii) the spiritual tradition operating within your school.
- Make a list of the core non-negotiable assumptions made by each of these traditions.
- In what ways might these assumptions be challenged by adherents of alternative spiritual traditions?

The problem of ideological representation lies at the very heart of the controversial nature of contemporary spirituality. Contrasting spiritual systems offering conflicting explanations of the ultimate meaning and purpose of life cannot all be correct. Even those who elect to negate spiritual difference by imposing a post-modern ideological framework on the material are not exempt from the fact that they are making a spiritual truth claim. It is a brute fact that some traditions offer spiritual options that are inappropriate, morally unacceptable and even just simply false. The search for spiritual truth cannot be separated from the reality of ideology. This observation applies as much to the spiritual traditions themselves as to the representation of such traditions in the classroom: both are open to the possibility of ideological distortion.

It follows that teachers are faced with a stark choice. Either they must accept responsibility for adjudicating between the various spiritual ideologies on offer by selecting the most appropriate one to induct pupils into and deciding the best way to represent it in the classroom, or they must elect to pass the responsibility on to the pupils themselves by allowing them to confront a variety of spiritual traditions and provide them with the skills necessary to begin to discriminate effectively between them.

Put somewhat starkly, the choice is between cultivating contented pigs or discontented philosophers. It is this critical edge that is frequently lacking in the current staple diet of an inclusive spirituality grounded in experiential relativism. If spiritual education is to be effective, then children must be taught to identify and respond effectively to the presence of ideology in spiritual discourse. There is no neutral ground, and the educator, in presenting a range of spiritual traditions, must enable children to recognise the fundamental axioms and presuppositions upon which contrasting spiritual traditions are founded. The need to confront ideological representation with critical thinking is the third of the five principles of critical spiritual education identified in this chapter.

Liberalism as an Interim Ethic

For many the model of critical pedagogy being developed here will appear distinctly illiberal: Does it not promise division rather than unity? Will it not cultivate conflict rather than mutual understanding? As we have already seen, such concerns are at the heart of Hull's programme of liberal spiritual education. This section argues that such concerns are unfounded, and that a genuinely liberal education must necessarily be a critical one.

Mark Halstead (1995) has identified three core liberal values: individual liberty, equality of respect, and consistent rationality, in other words, the principles of freedom, tolerance and reason. We are free to believe and behave as we like, provided we are (i) willing to tolerate the freedom of others to think and act as they choose, and (ii) seek to resolve any ensuing disputes through rational debate.

A significant feature of contemporary culture has been the rise of liberal fundamentalism, in the form of aggressive, authoritarian and 'politically correct' attempts to defend the liberal tradition by utilising – as a first rather than as a last resort – the distinctly anti-liberal methods of repression and censorship and by encouraging a policy of rigorous policing to ensure that all non-liberal positions are silenced. In adopting this strategy liberal fundamentalism actually undermines the very basis of liberalism by doing the following:

- ignoring liberalism's commitment to rational debate;
- undermining the liberal desire to tolerate genuine difference;
- making martyrs of those whose freedom of speech is subsequently curtailed;
- metamorphosing liberalism into a closed, non-negotiable – and hence fundamentalist – world-view.

When John Locke first invoked the liberal principles of freedom, tolerance and reason, he did so in the context of a society in danger of collapsing into anarchy. The principles were never intended by Locke to constitute a specific world-view, but rather to function as an interim ethic concerned to enhance the possibility of reasoned debate between conflicting ideological positions. As Nicholas Wolterstorff puts it, Locke was concerned to develop a *doxastic practice* through which communication between diverse traditions could be maximised (Wolterstorff, 1996). The historical roots of liberalism were ethical rather than ontological: they had little to do with constructing an alternative world-view, and everything to do with communication across cultural boundaries:

> It is to politics and not epistemology that we have to look ... (if we are to recover liberalism's) animating vision of a society in which persons of diverse traditions live together in justice and friendship, conversing with each other and slowly altering their traditions in response to their conversation.
>
> (ibid., p. 246)

Arguing along similar lines Graham Haydon suggests that liberal education should discard a hard notion of liberalism as a comprehensive world-view committed to its own distinctive beliefs and morality, in favour of a soft notion of liberalism as a provisional ethic:

> A society which tried to exclude anyone who was not a liberal in their moral outlook would be a markedly illiberal society ... The liberal educator has to

> promote the values that are necessary to living in a liberal society, but [should]
> stop short of promoting a liberal set of moral beliefs or lifestyle.
>
> (Haydon, 1997, p. 128)

Historically, liberalism has shown a commitment not merely to freedom, but also to tolerance of the 'other', particularly so in those situations where the 'other' is a distinctively illiberal cultural tradition: the mark of the liberal fundamentalist is their ability to tolerate only fellow liberals; the mark of the authentic liberal is their ability to tolerate non-liberals. This is not to suggest that there is no liberal 'bottom line': there is clearly a point at which liberals must be prepared to resist acts of intolerance that threaten the basic fabric of liberalism. However, given the principle of rationality, such resistance will always be a last resort, introduced only when all other attempts to broker a reasonable solution have failed.

This notion of liberalism as an interim ethic rather than a closed ontology illuminates the way in which Hull's premature retreat into educational censorship, as explored in the previous chapter, tends to approach liberalism as world-view rather than as an ethic of communication. Generally speaking, Hull's invocation of the twin principles of freedom and tolerance fails to do justice to the third liberal principle of reason. This leads him in the direction of an educational paternalism that seeks to enforce freedom and tolerance without the aid of educated reason and consequently finds itself at odds with the historical roots of liberalism.

Activity

- Is the distinction between liberalism as a 'world-view' and as an 'interim ethic' a valid one?
- Is there any truth in the suggestion that some elements of the liberal tradition have taken on fundamentalist traits?
- To what extent do the liberal attitudes operating in your educational institution offer an appropriate balance between the principles of freedom, tolerance and reason?

Critical education is, then, a requirement of liberalism rather than an optional extra. As Peter Hobson and John Edwards have argued, a liberal education-for-belief demands that we acquire our beliefs in a critical manner so that (i) our personal autonomy is not diminished, and ii) false or insufficiently understood beliefs do not become the cause of harm or injury to others in the community (Hobson and Edwards, 1999, pp. 85–104). The need to embrace liberalism as an interim ethic in which the freedom and tolerance are not separated from reason is the fourth of the five principles of critical spiritual education identified in this chapter.

A Process-Oriented Spiritual Pedagogy

A foundational spiritual education, such as the one currently in vogue in many schools, normally proceeds by isolating a specific definition of spirituality and then uses that definition as the foundation of its curriculum development. A process-based spiritual education begins by rejecting – in the light of the controversial nature of spirituality – the viability of establishing such a foundational definition and instead approaches spiritual education as an ongoing journey of exploration, one that is not dependent on any prior agreement about the nature of spirituality.

Such a process-oriented spiritual education operates within a shared educational space, in which the classroom functions as a type of educational 'chat room' within which communication between conflicting traditions may be facilitated. Entry into this learning site is unrestricted and does not require any prior agreement about the nature of spirituality. This is because a critical spiritual education that takes the ambiguity of spirituality seriously must be open to a diversity of spiritual perspectives, and cannot be true to itself if it proposes *a priori* solutions to spiritual problems.

Activity

- Is the distinction between 'foundational' and 'process' forms of spiritual education viable?
- What are the advantages and disadvantages of proceeding with an open-ended understanding of spirituality?
- To what extent does current practice in your school reflect either of these options?

The function of the shared space is to establish a site within which conflicting traditions are free to express themselves with impunity, safe from the fear of their individuality melting into an inclusive mishmash. The establishment of such a site does the following:

- opens up the possibility of educative exchanges between alternative spiritual traditions;
- actively resists the premature closure of debate
- provides a common space for learning
- encourages controversy, ambiguity and tension;
- facilitates conversation, dialogue and debate;
- stimulates the emergence of spiritual literacy.

The transformation of the classroom into a site for conversation between pupils and a variety of spiritual traditions enables a foundationalist education to be replaced by a process oriented education, and this constitutes the fifth of the five principles of critical spiritual education identified in this chapter.

Summary

In this chapter we have proposed five principles on which a critical spiritual education may be developed. These are:

- a challenge to the current malaise of spiritual education;
- a move beyond the intrinsic-extrinsic impasse;
- the development of critical awareness of ideology;
- an assimilation of liberalism as an interim ethic;
- the establishment of a process-oriented pedagogy.

10 An Agenda for Critical Spiritual Education

Critical spiritual education seeks to transcend the inclusive–exclusive impasse by acknowledging both the universality of our shared spiritual quest and the integrity of the specific traditions within which the quest is pursued. This requires a rich multi-dimensional presentation of spirituality which does not hesitate to embrace controversy. Such a presentation is possible only if the task of curriculum development is restructured. The paternalistic alternatives of searching for an all-inclusive common-denominator spirituality, and of pre-packaging a single exclusive spiritual tradition, lead only to cardboard one-dimensional representations. Rather than smoothing over the rough edges of spirituality prior to the start of the learning process, the complexity and ambiguity of spirituality needs to be tabled as an issue for direct exploration in the classroom. Spirituality, that is to say, must be treated as a controversial subject.

In the previous chapter we identified five principles from which such a critical pedagogy ought to proceed. In the present chapter the focus shifts from the framework of spiritual education to its material content. The aim is to propose an agenda to guide the educative conversations between pupils, teachers and a diverse range of spiritual traditions. This is done on the basis of a fresh definition of spirituality that deliberately sets out to challenge the inclusive status quo. The function of this new model is not to attempt to prematurely solve the problem of spirituality in a foundational manner, but rather to give an initial impetus to the ongoing process of spiritual pedagogy. The definition is thus intended as an opening gambit in the process of spiritual education, an attempt to articulate an initial starting point from which the exploration of spirituality can proceed. The definition serves to set an agenda in which the plurality of spiritual traditions are respected, the quest for spiritual truth takes centre stage and the overarching aim is to enhance children's levels of spiritual literacy.

Spirituality Redefined

Just like the inclusive model described in Chapter 7, the revised definition of spirituality presented here is concerned to be widely accepted across a broad range of spiritual opinion. However, unlike the inclusive model, it does not claim to identify any universal foundation of human spirituality. Instead the basis of its claim for general acceptance is more modest: it seeks merely to establish an initial starting point for spiritual conversation. As such, the revised model operates as a heuristic device, concerned not to impose spiritual truth claims, but to cultivate dialogue between conflicting traditions without compromising their unique identities. It is crucially important to recognise that an initial rejection of the definition does not make the model invalid, since by stimulating such objections it will already have served its purpose.

This, then, is the provisional definition of spirituality I wish to propose:

> Spirituality is the relationship of the individual, within community and tradition, to that which is – or is perceived to be – of ultimate concern, ultimate value and ultimate truth, as appropriated through an informed, sensitive and reflective striving for spiritual wisdom.

Though few adherents of a specific spiritual tradition are likely to be able to whole-heartedly accept the definition as it stands, the hope is that the vast majority will be able to make charitable use of it as a stepping stone to the articulation of their own specific formulations, and therefore as a stimulus for ongoing educational debate.

Activity

- Assess the strengths and weaknesses of the revised definition of spirituality.
- Match them to the situation in your school.

The model deliberately sets out to overcome three of the basic problems already identified as being inherent in the inclusive approach to spiritual pedagogy:

- *spiritual tradition* – it seeks to transcend the limitations of a spirituality of introspective experience by engaging with forms of spirituality embodied in historical, cultural, linguistic and social tradition;
- *spiritual truth* – it is concerned to resist the instinct to bracket out the question of the material content of spirituality by engaging directly with the question of spiritual truth;
- *spiritual wisdom* – it sets out to challenge raw unreflective spiritual emotivism by engaging with critical thinking.

Spiritual Tradition

It has already been noted how advocates of the inclusive model equate spirituality with an introspective sensibility rooted in the emotive exploration of our personal 'inner space' and independent of any specific spiritual tradition. Such a perspective is, however, open to question.

The commitment to introspection as a path to truth is closely associated with the individualistic anthropology cultivated by René Descartes. In his search for certainty and truth he set out systematically to doubt anything he might be tempted to place his trust in: God, tradition, society, nature, his body, logic, reason, and even his sanity. This 'hermeneutic of suspicion' increasingly dislocates Descartes from external reality, until finally there is only one thing that he is unable to doubt: the very fact that he is doubting: '*Cogito ergo sum*', 'I think, therefore I am'. Descartes' legacy to the modern world is the image of the isolated self, dislocated from communal tradition and reliant entirely on its own inner reason, feeling and experience. From this flows the commonly held romantic view that our ultimate values should be derived directly from the authority of our inner experiences, a position not far removed from the post-modern belief that we are free to construct our own personal spiritual realities.

There are, however, a number of reasons for placing a question mark over this entire way of looking at things.

Communal Language

The second half of the twentieth century saw a groundswell of opinion against this image of spirituality as the exploration of our 'inner space'. A lead was taken by the philosopher Ludwig Wittgenstein who, in his *Philosophical Investigations*, challenged the view that language operates ostensively by (i) naming objects in the physical world, and (ii) giving expression to our inner experiences (Wittgenstein, 1968). In both cases the picture of language presupposes Descartes' notion of the isolated self: it is precisely because we see ourselves as dislocated from reality that we try to use language either to re-connect ourselves with external reality, or to express our private inner feelings. Challenging this image, Wittgenstein invites us to accept a rich, multi-dimensional understanding of the way language operates:

> Our language can be seen as an ancient city, a maze of little streets and squares, of old and new houses, and of houses with additions from various periods: and this surrounded by a multitude of new boroughs with straight regular streets and uniform houses.
>
> (ibid., p. 8)

Wittgenstein's point here is that the modern cult of the individual has tended to work with simplistic and monolithic models of language, treating language as if it were as uniform and regular as the architecture of a modern housing estate. In reality, he suggests, language is a far more diverse and complicated affair, more like a city that, having developed over many centuries, embraces a rich diversity of contrasting architectural styles. This leads Wittgenstein to conclude that language is rooted in public communal traditions. We master language not by indulging in the private language game of naming our inner feelings, but by engaging with the diverse forms of life through which people communicate with one another and seek to make sense of the world. It follows that when we speak about ourselves and about other people we do so not in isolation, but as part of a web of language that binds us together as relational people.

105

Communal Science

This rediscovery of the communal nature of language has been reinforced by the demise of the 'spectator theory' of science. This now generally discredited theory advocates objectivity, freedom from prejudice and separation from external authority as the basis of scientific discovery. Rejecting the spectator theory, Thomas Kuhn argues that we learn to do science not by stepping back and seeking a neutral vantage point, but by immersing ourselves in the traditions of the scientific community (Kuhn, 1970):

> The account of science as an inherently social activity, carried out by collaboration in institutions which transmit and transform information from one generation to another, rules out the empiricist assumption that knowledge is essentially an individual product and possession.
>
> (Collier, 1994, p. 75)

The acquisition of knowledge is a social activity rather than an individual one: once again we are confronted with a vision of the communal nature of personhood.

Communal Hermeneutics

Gadamer rejects the assumption that neutrality – achieved through the suspension, or bracketing out, of our prejudice and pre-understanding – offers an appropriate path to understanding. On the contrary, he contends, we learn by anticipating meaning on the basis of our prior assumptions: 'A person who is trying to understand a text is always performing an act of projection' (Gadamer, 1979, p. 237). This, however, is not the same as allowing our prejudices to become authoritarian. We acknowledge them precisely in order to allow them to be challenged by new meaning and new truth. When our pre-understanding does not match with the truth claims in the book before us we encounter the 'experience of being pulled up short by the text' (ibid.). It is this dissonance between the horizon and the reader and the horizon of the text that draws the reader into fresh insight. Above all, Gadamer argues, we must cultivate sensitivity towards what we are trying to understand, since

> this kind of sensitivity involves neither 'neutrality' in the matter of the object nor the extinction of one's self, but the conscious assimilation of one's own bias, so that the text may be present itself in all its newness and thus able to assert its own truth against one's own fore-meanings.
>
> (ibid., p. 239)

It follows from this that the priority attributed to prejudice-free experience must be rejected. 'The fundamental prejudice of the Enlightenment is the prejudice against prejudice itself, which deprives tradition of its power' (ibid.). Genuine understanding demands not introspection but reflection on the community and tradition we indwell. 'Long before we understand ourselves through the process of self-examination, we understand ourselves in a self-evident way in the family, society and state in which we live' (ibid., p. 245).

Activity

'Personal identity is rooted not merely in our capacity for self-understanding but also in the nature of our developing relationship with others in community, with the natural world and with the presence or absence of God'.

Discuss this.

It is certainly not being suggested that we should simply ignore inner experience, merely that – in the light of our developing understanding of the language, scientific procedure and hermeneutical understanding – such experience will always be understood and interpreted in the light of the communities and traditions which have helped mould us into the people we are. The fact that personal identity is as dependent on communal relationships as it is on private introspection suggests the need for a spiritual pedagogy which takes account of the shared traditions of meaning through which our ultimate beliefs and values are expressed. It follows that critical spiritual education must take account of the specific traditions within which the spiritual has its home.

Spiritual Truth

The Eclipse of Truth

'Truth' is currently a deeply unfashionable concept that runs against the grain of the vogue for all things post-modern. The romantic stress on experience, in which truth is rooted in individual perception, suggests that at best truth is a relative concept: 'your truth' and 'my truth' are not necessarily the same thing. This relativism quickly slips into the post-modern deconstruction of all truth claims. In its strong form post-modernity claims that reality is itself essentially chaotic and impervious to all attempts at rational description. A softer version of the argument simply asserts that the question of whether reality is chaotic or not is beyond the limits of human comprehension: the question of truth is irrelevant, since we have no possible access to the answer.

The rise of relativism and the deconstruction of the question of truth have not been driven simply by academic questions of epistemology. There is an important moral dimension to the debate. In our post-colonial world we are all too familiar with the power structures embedded in authoritarian truth claims, and the ways in which they can lead to the repression and manipulation of disenfranchised minorities. In fact, the eclipse of questions of truth is inextricably linked to the affirmation of the liberal values of freedom and tolerance. In some quarters at least simply to make a truth claim constitutes an act of cultural repression, on the grounds that such an affirmation will inevitably be intolerant of alternative truth claims.

The Rehabilitation of Truth

The model of spirituality proposed above challenges the prevailing consensus. It draws directly from the twin sources of Socratic reasoning and Hebraic wisdom. The Socratic belief that the unexamined life is not worth living, that it is better to be a discontented philosopher than a contented pig, together with the Hebraic belief that our lives can be authentic only if lived in a proper relationship with the actual order of reality, are twin axioms taken for granted here.

But are not these twin principles simply anathema to post-modern forms of thought? I would like to suggest that they are not, on the grounds that the question of truth is unavoidable and inevitable, even for the staunch post-modernist. The post-modern philosopher who seeks to deconstruct the issue of truth is in fact making – at least implicitly – one of three possible truth claims: (i) the 'truth claim' that reality is inherently chaotic; (ii) the 'truth claim' that we are not competent to judge whether or not reality has a rational foundation; or (iii) the 'truth claim' that all truth claims are morally objectionable and hence should not be made.

Post-modernity, that is to say, is inextricably bound up with questions of truth, whether it recognises the fact or not. If any of these three assertions are correct, as indeed they might well be, then we ought – in true Socratic and Hebraic fashion – to respond responsibly to the situation and, following the advice of post-modern philosophers, adopt a life style appropriate to this post-modern reality. The key point is that, in electing to follow this option, we are implicitly accepting the validity and truth of post-modernity. At the end of the day the question of the relativism and deconstruction of the concept of truth is itself part and parcel of the struggle for truth.

Whether we affirm ourselves as a religious believer, and atheist or an agnostic; whether we see ourselves as a naturalist, a romantic, a post-modernist or a critical realist, the fact remains that we will inevitably find ourselves taking a stance in the broad spectrum of truth claims and counter-claims. There is simply no neutral ground available to us: relativistic epistemologies and deconstructive hermeneutics are not ways of transcending the question of truth, but rather moves within the ongoing search for truth.

The 'Epistemic Fallacy'

If we are forced to grapple with the question of truth then it is vital that we are aware of the dangers of the 'epistemic fallacy': the mistaken assumption that the way things are in the world are dependent on our ability to perceive them. Epistemology, our way of knowing the world, does not have priority over ontology, the way things are actually in the world. We have already seen how positivism falls into this trap in its fallacious argument that, since we cannot experience God through our physical senses, it follows that God does not exist. Similarly, the post-modern claim that we are not competent to judge whether reality is inherently rational does not justify the conclusion that the world is actually chaotic. In both cases premature conclusions about the nature of reality are drawn from the fact that our capacity to experience and reason has its limits, when in fact a reflective agnosticism would appear to be a more appropriate response. The quest for truth needs to recognise the crucial distinction between the way things are in the world and our ability to perceive the world.

It follows that we must accept the possibility that our ultimate values may not appropriately reflect the way things actually are in the world: if, for example, our spiritual beliefs are Christian ones, but the God of Christianity is merely a figment of our imagination, then our spiritual lives rest on a falsehood and we are condemned to live delusional spiritual lives out of harmony with the actual order of things. It is not an unreasonable conclusion to draw that a spiritual life integrated with the way things are in the world is preferable to a life dislocated from reality.

Truth and Linguistic Communities

Finally, the search for truth is normally a communal process. The notion that we begin our search for truth by rejecting all our cultural baggage and start out afresh without any prior assumptions is a naïve one. Collier points out that this 'clean slate fallacy' is both too radical and too conservative: it is too radical, since the wisdom of the past is arrogantly swept aside; and it is too conservative, because it encourages a naïve and uncritical reliance on our own thought and experience. What is needed is a critical respect for both our tradition and our experience: 'we cannot think for ourselves productively until we have had long practice in thinking other people's thoughts after them' (Collier, 1994, p. 71). Spiritual literacy demands that we engage with forms of public discourse rather than simply relying on our own resources. Just as 'a person with no ornithological vocabulary sees only birds, not pied wagtails or dunnocks,' so a person with no spiritual vocabulary encounters only raw untutored emotion (ibid.).

Activity

- How convincing do you find the case made out above for the inevitability and centrality of the question of spiritual truth in education?
- What difference does it make that, in the public sphere at least, all such spiritual truth will have the status of provisional judgement rather than verifiable fact?

Despite the fact that questions of truth are currently out of vogue, the question of spiritual truth is unavoidable, and the relationship between the way we perceive ultimate reality and the way ultimate reality actually is in itself is of fundamental importance to our communal search for the ultimate meaning and purpose of life.

Spiritual Wisdom

A common criticism of critical spiritual education is that it entails a rationalism that does not do justice to the affective dimension of spiritual experience. Such criticism has close links with romantic and post-modern attacks on the tyranny of reason. By imposing rational thought forms on pupils in the classroom, so the argument goes, we undermine their capacity for authentic spiritual experience. However, the commitment of critical spiritual education is not to rationalism but to wisdom.

The 'Dissociation of Sensibility'

This basic contrast between the domains of the rational and the emotive is emerging as a key issue for contemporary spirituality. It reflects a dualistic trait in modern Western thought that relies on a series of binary opposites: fact/value, knowledge/belief, objectivity/subjectivity, reason/emotion, sense/sensibility. Commentators whose unease with critical spiritual education is expressed through their preference for the immediacy of emotive experience over against abstract rationalism, are clearly operating within this dualistic structure. However, the present advocacy of spiritual wisdom does not entail a preference for the rational over the affective, but rather constitutes an attempt to transcend a false and unnecessary polarity.

The poet and critic T.S. Eliot famously described this dualistic contrast between reason and feeling as the 'dissociation of sensibility'. A key feature of modern literature, he suggests, has been the dislocation of thought from feeling in which the flip side of a crude academic rationalism is an unrefined emotivism. In the process both our sense and our sensibility suffer (a theme explored in Jane Austen's *Sense and Sensibility*). Translating this dissociation of sensibility to the realm of spiritual education leads to a false choice between a spirit-negating rationalism and an untutored emotivism.

Personal Knowledge

Michael Polanyi (1958) has pioneered the notion of a 'personal knowledge' which seeks to overcome this dissociation of sensibility by transforming our impersonal and mechanistic modes of rationality. He argues that the 'personal is not a hindering factor but the intelligent centre of knowledge' (Gelwick, 1977, pp. 47f.). We must learn to see passionate involvement rather than objective detachment as the foundation of insight and understanding. Personal knowledge brings the subjective and the objective together into a creative whole in which our vision of the universe is driven by the unity of feeling and reason, imagination and reflection. Such a vision is for Polanyi essentially realistic, committed to an engagement with a reality beyond our subjective imagination. The fact that we engage imaginatively with reality does not entitle us to drop basic critical standards of investigation in favour of the creation of an imaginary make-believe world.

Knowledge cannot be reduced to the level of facts in an objective and personally irrelevant world. Neither can knowledge be limited to self-awareness, self-affirmation and the cultivation of fantasy. The search for knowledge is simultaneously the search for an appropriate relationship with the reality we find ourselves thrown into. Our striving after realistic knowledge runs hand in hand with our striving for self-formation. This identification of knowledge with wisdom, is encapsulated in the German term *Bildung*:

[T]his word signifies two processes: learning and personal growth. They are not understood apart from one another, as if education were only a means to growth. Rather learning is taken to be constitutive of personal development, as part and parcel of how we become a human being in general and a specific individual in particular.

(Beiser, 1998, p. 286)

As Gadamer points out, *Bildung*

designates primarily the proper human way of developing one's natural talents and capacities ... the attitude of mind which, from the knowledge and feeling of the total moral and intellectual endeavour, flows harmoniously into sensibility and character ... it consists in learning to allow what is different from oneself and to find universal viewpoints from which one can grasp the thing ... without selfish interest.

(1979, pp. 10ff.)

This notion of personal knowledge as *Bildung*, or self-formation, through our developing relationship with the world, brings us directly to the issue of wisdom.

Critical Wisdom

Nicholas Maxwell (1987) argues the need for a revolution across all our academic and educational enterprises that will transform our intellectual aims and methods of inquiry. 'At present inquiry is devoted to the enhancement of knowledge', but 'this needs to be transformed into a kind of rational inquiry having as its basic aim to enhance personal and social wisdom' (ibid., p. v). We have to learn to give 'intellectual priority to the personal and social problems we encounter in our lives as we strive to realise what is desirable and of value', and so cultivate a 'tradition of genuinely rational social thought, devoted to the growth of wisdom' (ibid.).

Maxwell understands wisdom as 'the desire, the active endeavour, and the capacity to discover and achieve what is of value, the ability to see what is of value, actually and potentially, in the circumstances of life' (ibid., p. 66). 'The basic task of rational inquiry is to help develop wiser ways of living, wiser institutions, customs and social relations' (ibid.). Crucial here is the recognition that wisdom and knowledge cannot be separated. To be wise is to embark on a process of self-formation through a personal engagement with the world we indwell, an engagement that transcends the misplaced dissociation of sense from sensibility, feeling from reason.

Activity

- Do you agree with the suggestion that the division between rational sense and emotive sensibility is an unnecessary one?
- How coherent do you find the vision of a critical wisdom rooted in *Bildung* and personal knowledge?

Summary

The chapter aimed at setting an agenda for critical spiritual education, concluding that spiritual literacy is likely to be enhanced if teaching focuses on three issues:

- the integrity of the various traditions within which human spiritual under-standing is embodied;
- the question of spiritual truth, embodying not merely human concerns about the ultimate meaning and purpose of life, but also of the ultimate nature of reality;
- a critical wisdom that transcends the modernist polarity of rationalistic sense and emotive sensibility.

11 Spiritual Education as Nurture

The principles outlined in Chapter 9, together with the agenda proposed in Chapter 10, provide a starting point for a critical spiritual education. The present chapter, together with the following one, will explore two complementary approaches to learning, both of which are essential for the establishment of spiritual literacy. An effective spiritual education, it will be suggested, must be equally committed to education as nurture and education as critique.

This chapter will focus on the process of spiritual nurture, defending the thesis that spiritual education ought to consciously and intentionally ground pupils in a specific spiritual tradition, as identified, articulated and owned by the school community. The chapter begins with a brief outline of the historical tradition that views education as a process of cultural transmission. It is then suggested, somewhat controversially, that indoctrination is both a necessary and inevitable component of effective spiritual education. Every school has a responsibility to nurture pupils into a broad set of shared national spiritual values, as well as into the values of its own specific spiritual tradition, a process that carries with it clear implications for the development of school ethos and Collective Worship.

Such a notion of education as cultural transmission is, of course, a deeply unfashionable one in many educational circles. I would urge those who anticipate struggling with the views expressed in this chapter to approach it in the light of the liberal principle of charitable openness, and to constantly bear in mind that educational nurture remains a wholly inadequate option unless supplemented with the critical pedagogy presented in Chapter 12.

Education as Cultural Transmission

The notion that schools should be responsible for transmitting cultural and spiritual norms reflects a deeply rooted historical understanding of the proper function of education. Though extremely unpopular in many contemporary educational circles it draws support from many politicians, parents and social commentators, and clearly resonates with popular public sentiment.

The *Concise Oxford Dictionary* offers the following definition of indoctrination: 'teach (a person or group) systematically or for a long period to accept (esp. partisan or tendentious) ideas uncritically'. However, the pejorative use of the word is of comparatively recent origin, and traditionally a good teacher was simply an effective indoctrinator, since to indoctrinate was to do no more than teach or instruct. The root meaning of indoctrination is simply to 'inculcate the doctrine' or 'pass on the truth', and the transmission of common public truth represented an established educational norm expected of all teachers. However, the reality of cultural pluralism, coupled with a commitment to the principles of freedom and tolerance, has led modern educators to view the process of indoctrination with suspicion. Following the success in the twentieth century of totalitarian forms of education, of which the methods of the Hitler Youth Movement have become a paradigmatic example, it is no longer possible to disguise the potentially authoritarian nature of indoctrination. There is now widespread concern that, in the absence of public consensus, indoctrinatory teaching methods impose as 'true' values and dogmas that are in reality no more than mere 'opinion'. This modern suspicion of indoctrination masks the reality that historically education as the transmission of culture has consistently been the norm rather than the exception.

The Judaeo-Christian-Islamic and Classical Traditions

The monotheistic traditions of Judaism, Christianity and Islam, which have played a significant role in shaping Western education, have always been closely associated with nurture and indoctrination. In Hebrew scripture, for example, the history of God's covenantal relationship with his chosen people, especially as this is embodied in the Torah, is to be faithfully transmitted from generation to generation:

> These commandments which I give you this day are to be remembered and taken to heart: teach them to your children, and speak of them both indoors and out of doors, when you lie down and when you get up.
>
> (Deuteronomy 6:4f.)

In the Classical tradition of the Graeco-Roman world, and especially in the pedagogical thinking of Aristotle, we encounter a similar understanding of education as cultural transmission. Aristotle understands happiness as the highest spiritual goal available to humanity, and holds that, since we are essentially social creatures, our achievement of happiness is dependent on the cultivation of responsible citizenship: 'happiness (*eudaimonia*), interwoven as it is with that of ... wives, children, friends, and fellow citizens, is a communal achievement' (Reeve, 1998, p. 51). Consequently education must be fundamentally concerned with transmitting normative standards of belief, virtue and behaviour upon which stable community life is dependent.

> The goal of an Aristotelian education of the appetites and emotions, then, is to produce citizens with the virtues and the conceptions of happiness suited to their constitution, citizens for whom acting in accord with the laws is second nature, it having seeped into their characters like dye into wool.
>
> (ibid., p. 57)

John Locke: Some Thoughts Concerning Education

It is perhaps surprising that, with the dawning of the Enlightenment and its spirit of criticism, we do not encounter an immediate rejection of education as cultural transmission. John Locke, one of the founders of modern British educational thought, offered his vision of education in *Some Thoughts Concerning Education* (Locke, 1968). This series of letters to Edward Clarke, advising him on the upbringing of his son, presents an approach to education marked by an atmosphere of realism, pragmatism and utilitarianism. Locke is concerned to enable Clarke to mould his son into a model of the bourgeoisie liberal English gentleman, for whom 'a sound mind in a sound body, is a short, but full description of a happy state in this world' (ibid., p. 114). At the heart of Locke's educational policy is the cultivation of character, understood as a disciplined mind and body grounded in the public virtues of civility, love of justice, courage and humanitarianism.

Locke has a high view of the power of education: 'of all men we meet with, nine parts of ten are what they are, good or evil, useful or not, by their education' (ibid.). He suggests that the child must develop a capacity for self-discipline, inculcated through the authority and guidance of his tutor, whose influence is progressively relaxed as self-mastery is achieved. Locke works with a psychology of learning that may best be described as a form of benign behaviourism, in which reward and punishment are central to the learning process, though always implemented in such a fashion as to promote a happy disposition rather than slavish obedience. It is the authority of the tutor, and his (sic) ability to mould and form the minds of their pupils, upon which successful education depends. 'Great care is to be had of the forming of children's minds, and the giving them that seasoning early, which shall influence their lives always after' (ibid., p. 138).

Locke's understanding of education as the cultivation of character through the transmission of moral and cultural norms draws on both the Judaeo-Christian and Classical traditions. It quickly became the foundation of mainstream educational thinking, forming the basis of the educational philosophy of the public school system, and later providing a model for state sponsored grammar and comprehensive schools. Both the 1944 and 1988 Education Acts assume that education has a primary responsibility to form character through the transmission of cultural traditions, norms and values. In the history of Western education the basic principle of education as cultural transmission has consistently been the established norm.

The Value of Indoctrination

Why then the contemporary resistance to education as cultural transmission? We have already alluded to the primary cause: in a pluralistic society the question as to which set of traditions should be transmitted is inevitably the subject of fundamental disagreement. As a result education as cultural transmission is open to the charge of complicity in the ideological imposition of authoritarian discourse and forms of knowledge.

> Discourses are about what can be said and what can be thought, but also about who can speak, when, and with what authority ... the dominant discourses are often so powerful that the dissenter finds it hard to voice dissent articulately or objectively.
>
> (Gold and Evans, 1998, p. 9; Ball, 1990, p. 2)

It is tempting to limit the scope of such cultural imperialism to reactionary elements of the right-wing of British society seeking to impose traditional bourgeoisie, white, male, middle-class, quasi-Christian values on our children. However, it is important to recognise that the power base in education is not exclusively owned by the political right, and that left-wing ideology underpins much of the educational discourse concerning issues of multiculturalism, anti-racism, gay rights, equal opportunities, etc. The issue here – and this cannot be stressed enough – has nothing to do with the rights and wrongs of the conflicting educational agendas of left and right. The point I am seeking to make is simply that both a right-wing-inspired citizenship education and a left-wing-inspired anti-homophobic education are likely to adopt similar educational methods, using the process of cultural transmission to inculcate a set of values and behavioural norms in pupils. The dispute between left and right cannot simply be characterised by a choice between right-wing indoctrination and left-wing freedom, but rather takes the form of a power struggle, with the victors winning the right to indoctrinate their own value system in the classroom. It is increasingly difficult to adhere to the 'myth of neutrality': in a pluralistic society there is no neutral space, since one person's truth is always another person's ideological distortion.

Activity

- Make a list of the core values transmitted by your school: both explicitly through the curriculum and implicitly through its general ethos.
- Is it true that education will inevitably transmit a set of values and that consequently indoctrination is inevitable and neutrality impossible?

In this situation, schools need to accept that they will inevitably be party to the ideological transmission of cultural values and norms. The notion of education as cultural transmission is not a process schools can choose to opt out of. On the contrary, all education, whether positively or negatively, implicitly or explicitly, by intention or by default, will end up passing on a set of values and cultural norms to pupils.

It follows that the current suspicion of education as cultural transmission needs to be challenged. If such a process is indeed inevitable, then there can be no logical reason for objecting to it. Further, it makes sense for schools to acknowledge the inevitable and ensure that their best efforts are directed towards ensuring that the material content of the culture they choose to transmit, and the means by which they choose to transmit it, are carefully thought through, and offer children the best possible induction into the culture heritage of the tradition or traditions owned by the school community as a whole.

By identifying and publicly owning their prior ideological commitments schools will be better able to acknowledge, celebrate and enthusiastically transmit the values and world-views they are committed to. This is all the more important if the Qualifications and Curriculum Authority (QCA) is correct in claiming that (un-referenced) 'research shows that pupils can be keenly aware of discrepancies between values stated and values practised, and that such inconsistencies can lead to scepticism about the values shared' (QCA, 1999a, p. 7). If nurture is inevitable, then it must be done well, and this is unlikely to happen if a school, especially one hiding behind the myth of cultural neutrality, remains secretive and hesitant about its ulti-mate commitments and concerns.

A further reason for clearly identifying the underlying values of a school community is that a major step in challenging ideology lies in its unveiling. The more a school is up-front about its values and their source, the more likely it is that pupils, teachers, parents and the local community will be able to gain a critical perspective on the traditions upon which the school is grounded. The decision to be secretive and clandestine about a school's fundamental values is likely to perpetuate ideolog-ical distortion.

Education as cultural transmission is, then, an inevitable aspect of schooling, yet all such transmission will necessarily be open to the criticism of ideological represen-tation. The appropriate path beyond this dilemma is the explicit identification, articulation, celebration and transmission of the ultimate spiritual values that underpin the life of the school. If a school must transmit ideology, then it might as well transmit the very best available.

Structural Pluralism

If schools are to accept responsibility for identifying the spiritual foundations for their communal life and work, then inevitably the issue of its nature and content has to be asked. Once again we are brought back to the tension between inclusive and exclusive approaches to spirituality. Should a school opt for an all-embracing universal perspective, or should it adopt the viewpoint of a distinctive spiritual tradi-tion? Any answer to this question needs to take account of structural changes that have taken place in education following the 1988 Education Reform Act. The ideal of a common comprehensive education for all has given way to a structural pluralism that celebrates pedagogical diversity and supports a plurality of different types of schooling.

The emergence of structural pluralism is the result of the demise of the Local Education Authorities and the polarisation of power in education, both upwards to central government and downwards to individual schools. It is central government that, through legislation and non-statutory advice, sets the agenda for education, establishing its goals, processes, content and future direction. The ability of schools to conform to these demands and expectations has become the subject of a centralised regime of accountability, inspection, monitoring and control. The flip-side of this process of centralisation has been increasing levels of organisational, managerial and financial freedom enjoyed by individual schools, which has in turn led to a significant diversification of the range of available types of school.

The emergence of structural pluralism is of fundamental significance for spiritual education, since it is now the responsibility of the individual school to identify its own specific spiritual roots and establish its distinctive spiritual identity. Under current legislation schools are required by law to include an 'ethos statement' in the school prospectus. This means that interested parties can quite legitimately expect a school to articulate its fundamental values and ultimate spiritual concerns.

The ethos statement should reflect agreement between teachers and governors, parents and the local communities, who together constitute what is often a diverse school community, regarding the unity of values and purpose identified or established between them. Such shared values will provide the atmosphere of the school and underpin its life and work. The ethos established by these shared values will form the basis of the school's commitment to the spiritual, moral, social and cultural development of each pupil.

QCA's draft document offering schools curriculum guidance on Personal, Social, Health and Citizenship Education at Key Stages 1 and 2 defines values as 'the principles and criteria we use for judging what is good, worthwhile, desirable and right' (QCA 1999a, p. 7). Such values are not normally free-floating; they are likely to be rooted in our 'beliefs about ourselves, the world, life and reality, including moral codes and religious beliefs' (ibid.). QCA is clear that 'for many schools the ethos will be rooted in the religious beliefs and values associated with the origin of the school' (ibid.). This is significant, since QCA is pointing schools in the direction of identifying not just general moral principles, but the specific spiritual world-views that underpin the communal life of the school.

Activity

- examine a copy of your school's ethos statement.
- Is it possible to identify a clear spiritual vision concerning the ultimate meaning and purpose of life?
- Does the statement provide a fair reflection of the ongoing spiritual life of the school?

The polarity of central and local power bases in education, which reflect the tensions between inclusive and exclusive approaches to spirituality, mean inevitably that a school's ethos statement must take account of both the school's identity as part of a national system of education, and its identity as a unique local community. The school's ethos statement, functioning as the foundation of education as nurture and cultural transmission, will need to take account of both shared national values and local spiritual traditions.

Shared National Values

But what precisely do we mean by 'shared national values'? This question was addressed directly by the SCAA-sponsored conference, *Education for Adult Life*, which was convened in London in January 1996. The conference reflected a widespread concern to balance an academic curriculum with a broader education able to promote spiritual, moral, social and cultural development. As Nick Tate observes, nobody 'wants their child to leave school clutching a handful of certificates, but no idea of how to be a human being' (Talbot and Tate, 1997, p. 2).

The conference recommended the setting up of the Forum on Values in Education and the Community, which subsequently met in 1997. Its brief was twofold: (i) to discover whether there are any common values upon which agreement can be reached across the broad spectrum of society, and to which all could subscribe irrespective of race, ethnic group, religion, gender or class' (ibid); and (ii) to decide how best to support schools in the task of promoting spiritual, moral, social and cultural development. The resulting statement of four common values was subsequently included in the 1999 *National Curriculum Handbooks for Primary and Secondary Teachers*. The values are as follows:

- *The self* – We value ourselves as unique human beings capable of spiritual, moral, intellectual and physical growth and development.
- *Relationships* – We value others, not only for what they have or what they can do for us. We value relationships as fundamental to the development and fulfilment of ourselves and others, and to the good of the community.
- *Society* – We value truth, freedom, justice, human rights, the rule of law and collective effort for the common good. In particular, we value families as sources of love and support for all their members, and as the basis of a society in which people care for others.
- *The environment* – We value the environment, both natural and shaped by humanity, as the basis of life and a source of wonder and inspiration.

(Talbot and Tate, 1997, pp. 10–14)

Tate accepts that the results of the search for a common set of national values, one capable of being accepted by as wide a spectrum of society as possible, may be seen as rather bland and unspectacular

> of course the values once stated, appear obvious, of course they smack of apple pie and motherhood: anything as fundamental as this, once stated, will appear obvious. This doesn't make it any less true. If the Forum had come up with anything controversial it would not have been doing its job.

(ibid., p. 3)

Society, he suggests, has been so used to emphasising difference and celebrating moral relativity that it has failed to recognise the reality of common national values. The diverse backgrounds of the 150 members of the Forum, the widespread acceptance of the Forum's conclusions by a range of religious and secular groups, together with a Mori Poll indicated 95 per cent support among the public, combine to suggest that a set of shared values has indeed been identified. Tate is quick to make clear that these are values most of us already agree with, rather than values the Government wishes to impose on the nation. As the Statement of Values itself points out, 'the only authority claimed for these values, accordingly, is the authority of consensus' (ibid., p. 10).

Activity

- Examine the statement of shared values in the *National Curriculum Handbooks for Primary and Secondary Teachers*.
- Brainstorm your response to the statement.
- Which values do you find acceptable?
- Is there anything you object to?
- What is missing from the statement?
- Do the Handbooks fulfil their function of providing a set of shared values which teachers need not be apologetic about transmitting to pupils?

It is significant that the values articulated by the Forum have been challenged from both sides of the educational spectrum. Adrian Thatcher, writing from a Christian perspective, suggests that though the values may seem superficially attractive to Christians they fall short of being specifically Christian since they are not grounded in a Christian world-view (Thatcher, 1999b). In contrast, John Beck argues that Tate's strategy is little more than an attempt at closet Christian indoctrination, rooted in traditional models of Christian nurture (Beck, 1999). Both commentators seem to miss the point here: Thatcher is right that the values are not intrinsically Christian, but wrong to expect that they should be; Beck is unnecessarily reactionary in his identification of a hidden Christian agenda, ignoring the widespread approval of the values across the spectrum of religious and secular opinion.

The Values Forum is clear about the status of its common values: they are not intended to be foundational; they do not claim ontological significance; they are not rooted in any specific world view or spiritual tradition. Instead, the values constitute a set of provisional values that, operating as an interim ethic, seek to establish mutuality within a pluralist society without prejudice to the integrity of specific traditions and systems of belief. As the Preamble to the Values Statement makes clear, 'agreement on the values ... is compatible with disagreement on their sources' (Talbot and Tate, 1997, p. 3).

If this is so then both the significance and limitations of the work of the Forum become clear. Its significance lies in the identification of a set of national values that establish a shared space within which men and women from a diverse range of secular and religious traditions can gather with impunity. Its limitations lie in the fact that the values do no more than set the context within which the search for spiritual literacy can take place and do not go on to grapple with the specifics of distinct spiritual traditions. It follows that while a school may elect to adopt these broad national values in its ethos statement, this cannot be taken as a substitute for the task of identifying and articulating its particular spiritual values.

Local Spiritual Traditions

If schools are to hold fast to their spiritual integrity they must acknowledge their spiritual roots. To achieve this they will need to move beyond the affirmation of generalised value statements and articulate the specific world-view within which the school is operating. Part of the school's spiritual ethos, once identified, may well involve the adoption of the fourfold vision of the Values Forum. However, this will no longer be in the form of an interim ethic, since the values will now have been assimilated and restated within the framework of specific spiritual tradition upon which the school is founded. In many schools this may simply be an open-ended advocacy of liberalism, grounded in the recognition that a diverse range of spiritual traditions operate within the school, and that the concern of the school is to embrace a spirituality designed to allow all traditions to flourish alongside one another. Other schools may wish to adopt the spiritual vision of a specific religious tradition. Whatever the case, the key issue is that schools consciously and explicitly accept ownership of their spiritual foundations. In establishing and implementing an ethos statement schools will need to attend to a number of issues:

- *Identification of spiritual foundations* – the integrity of a school's spiritual life will be dependent upon the honest acknowledgement of its spiritual foundations. The days of a Church of England school evasively justifying its existence on the grounds that it is a 'caring community' (as if secular schools somehow fail in this area), rather than through its commitment to the rich tradition of Anglican theology, ought to be a thing of the past. Similarly a secular humanistic school which has self-consciously opted to bracket out questions of religious belief ought to bite the bullet and seek exemption from Collective Worship rather than continue with the farce of a daily act of worship which has little meaning within the community.
- *Attentiveness to the wider community* – if a school has a responsibility for asserting its own distinctive spiritual vision, it also has a duty to ensure that the way this vision interacts with the outside community, at local, regional and national level is properly thought through and practised. The affirmation of a school's identity should never be an excuse for sectarianism.
- *Openness to internal diversity* – the problems of achieving agreement within an individual school may be as challenging as the problems experienced at national level. Any school seeking to identify its spiritual world-view will need to take account of the power structures operating within its community, and be open to the possibility of genuine spiritual diversity. This may be diversity across the religious and secular spectrum, or in the case of faith community schools diversity within the different constituencies of a specific religious tradition. A Church of England school may need to take account of catholic, evangelical and liberal expressions of Anglican spirituality, as well as the presence of atheists, agnostics and adherents of alternative religious traditions within the community. Similarly,

a school committed to a form of secular humanism may need to be sensitive and responsive to the needs of minority Muslim pupils. Every school, whatever its foundation, will need to recognise the needs of all members of the community, balancing the concerns of the many with the needs of the few.

- *Collective ownership* – the spiritual roots of the community will need to be public property, articulated and owned by the school community. Research shows 'that a school where the purpose of education is clearly articulated and communicated is a far more effective school than one in which there is no obviously agreed purpose, or where the headteacher's view of education and schooling is not informed by and transmitted to the other people who work there (Gold and Evans, 1998, p. 14).

Activity

- Rewrite your school's ethos statement, taking account of the following factors:
    - (i) the need to articulate clear spiritual foundations;
    - (ii) the need to retain a positive relationship with the wider (pluralistic) community;
    - (iii) the need to be open to the diversity of spiritual opinions present within the school community;
    - (iv) the need to ensure that the ethos statement is owned by the whole school community.

Collective Worship

Finally, we must address a crucial, though frequently neglected, dimension of the spiritual life of the whole school: Collective Worship.

The sociologist Emile Durkheim (1858–1917) argued that religion is not merely concerned with beliefs and doctrine, but also with communal ritual, practice, and ceremony. Worship functions to identify and celebrate the common bonds between members of the religious community. In his classic study *The Elementary Forms of the Religious Life* (1971) Durkheim offers an analysis of the social functions of religion, showing how totemic objects act as symbols representing the origins of society, and how they serve to reinforce communal identity by drawing a distinction between the sacred and the profane. Religious worship works to mediate tensions within society, uniting members around shared symbols and thereby generating social solidarity.

> Durkheim proposes that the ritual and doctrinal distinctions between sacred and profane perform a vital social function in balancing the inherent tensions of every society between structure and counter-structure, order and chaos, morality and deviance, gathered tribe and dispersed hunter, or community and individual … Religion unites the members of a society around a common symbolic account

of their place in the cosmos, their history and purpose in the order of things ... he speculates that modern societies would need to develop rituals and symbol systems with which to generate a sense of solidarity in the new project of repub-licanism.

(Northcott, 1999, p. 196)

We have dwelt at length on Durkheim's interpretation of religious ritual because, for all its acknowledged faults, it identifies a key feature of the spiritual health of any community, namely, its ability to celebrate and share common achievements and ultimate concerns. Durkheim's insight is all the more significant in our contempo-rary individualistic and atomistic society in which, all too often, personal identity is rooted in solipsistic introspection rather than communal relationship. If the mark of a healthy spiritual society is its openness towards the celebration of its ultimate concerns and values, then it has to be said that many schools today are lacking in spiritual health. A partial, often cynical, attempt to appease OFSTED inspectors through an act of 'mainly Christian' worship with which only a minority can iden-tify and about which few have any ultimate concern, let alone interest, introduces a spiritual vacuum in the very heart of the school community. If a school accepts the responsibility of identifying and articulating its core spiritual values, then it also has a responsibility to ensure that these values are celebrated with dignity and integrity.

Activity

- What are the strengths and weaknesses of your school's programme of Collective Worship or shared assembly?
- Does it genuinely celebrate the spiritual life of the school?
- Describe the attitudes of staff and pupils towards the programme.
- In your opinion, what changes, if any, ought to be made?

Such celebration may take the form of either a religious act of Collective Worship or a secular assembly. It is worth noting that many critics of the current legislation regarding Collective Worship consistently fail to acknowledge its in-built flexibility and accept the diverse range of religious and secular options it makes available. The failure to take up an option appropriate to the specific spiritual foundation of the school is likely to be the result of a lack of will on the part of the school's leadership, rather than the result of legislation. A school committed to a secular spiritual tradition is not justified in criti-cising the imposition of Collective Worship until it has taken up its right to apply for an exemption from this particular part of the legislation.

Rather than constituting a necessary ill best delegated downwards to a willing, if unsuspecting, junior member of staff, Collective Worship or communal assembly ought to form the backbone of the spiritual life of the school community.

Summary

- The process of nurture culture constitutes a vital dimension of spiritual education.
- In a pluralistic society the ideological transmission of culture is inevitable, so schools ought to seek to transmit the very best culture available to them.
- The foundation of effective nurture is a clearly articulated and implemented ethos statement.
- An ethos statement must take account of national concerns regarding basic values, as well as the specific local concerns of the school's foundational spiritual tradition.
- Central to the spiritual life of any school community will need to be either Collective Worship or a common assembly.

12 Spiritual Education as Critique

Though education as nurture is a vital part of the learning process it remains open to abuse and constantly in danger of collapsing into the authoritarian imposition of a particular world-view. Consequently, the nurturing of pupils constitutes only one dimension of spiritual education, one which must be supplemented by the complementary process of education as critique. It is vital in our modern pluralistic society that we equip pupils with the ability to think for themselves and encourage them to take personal responsibility for their thoughts and actions. In the context of spiritual education this involves children developing the ability to live flourishing and virtuous spiritual lives, sensitive to their ultimate values and responsive to the ultimate values of those around them. This requires the cultivation of appropriate levels of spiritual literacy and autonomy that spiritual nurture alone cannot provide.

This suggestion of a reciprocal relationship between education as nurture and education as critique challenges the standard polarisation of traditionalist and progressive education. It identifies a third way between the extremes of traditionalist authoritarianism and progressive anarchy: the pedagogy of faith and the pedagogy of suspicion need not be mutually exclusive. Teaching concerned to induct children into a received cultural tradition and teaching concerned to cultivate the habit of critical autonomy may be seen as complementary processes.

This chapter begins by rejecting the false polarisation between progressive and traditionalist forms of education and goes on to abandon 'negative', 'deconstructive' and 'supplementary' models of learning in favour of 'reflective emancipation' or 'critical empowerment' as an appropriate foundation for the critical dimension of spiritual education. Such a critical education will be rooted in a search for truth that accepts the controversial nature of spirituality.

Progressive and Traditionalist Education

For many the celebration of education as a process of nurture set out in the previous chapter will have been unpalatable reading. Did it not advocate the transmission of a reactionary ideology intrinsically bound up with the vested interests of those in power? Was it not yet another example of the current ascendancy of a traditionalist educational rhetoric purveyed by the QCA and politicians across the political spectrum? Is not education as nurture simply the utilisation of schooling as a means of promoting social stability, a process that was central to the agenda of the previous Conservative administration, and which is fast becoming an educational reality through New Labour's advocacy of Citizenship Education?

Erricker Versus Tate

For Erricker such notions of citizenship are 'wedded to ideas of nationhood and Christian values' (Erricker *et al.*, 1997, p. 4). He reminds his readers that Nick Tate, in his position as the head of QCA, has affirmed the 'need to transmit a cultural heritage in schools which is rooted in Greece and Rome and in Christianity' (ibid., p. 184). Erricker doubts whether such an induction of children into the values and norms of white middle-class Christendom can genuinely bind together a profoundly pluralistic society and suggests that Tate has failed to address the question: 'whose society are we talking about and whose values does this "society" represent?' (ibid.). The 'results of such rhetoric', claims Erricker, 'are most likely to reinforce the very divisions we need to reconcile, and will do so by seeking to affirm power structures based on those divisions' (Erricker and Erricker, 1999, p. 130).

For Erricker the language of the educational traditionalist is rooted in fear of the threat posed by the 'other': traditionalism is inherently conservative and instinctively resistant to alternative viewpoints, cultures and lifestyles which depart from the perceived norm. Traditionalists, he argues, are unwilling to take either the psychological risk of embracing an education that might lead to children's self-transformation, or the political risk of an education that might lead to a transformation of the power structures of society. Erricker is clearly on the side of educational progressivism, putting his weight behind progressive movements which recognise the integrity of the whole child, and challenging those who would reduce education simply to the induction of children into adult society. This belief, that authentic education must preserve the child's autonomy rather than impose an external authoritarian adult morality, assumes a necessary polarisation between progressivism and traditionalism.

Rousseau's Romantic Pedagogy

Erricker's stance is, of course, not new. The romantic tradition of progressive child-centred education – which flourished in the 1960s before being eclipsed by the current vogue for back-to-basics traditionalism – can be traced back at least as far as Jean-Jacques Rousseau (1712–1778). Rousseau's pedagogy, shaped by the romantic reaction to modern rationalism, insists on the primacy of the child's autonomy over against the moribund culture norms of Enlightenment society (Rousseau, 1986). He sees the cultivation of children's autonomy as the means of preserving their natural goodness from corruption and advocates personal freedom as the only viable foundation for an authentic moral life. In direct opposition to the conservatism of John Locke, Rousseau believes that education must be concerned to protect children from the imposition of an alien authoritarian culture. Rejecting the Christian doctrine of the fall of humanity he argues that 'the first impulses of nature are always right; there is no original sin in the human heart' (ibid., p. 56). Children are born innocent and free, only to be corrupted by a depraved society as they grow into adulthood: 'everything is good as it comes from the hands of the maker of things; everything degenerates in the hands of man' (ibid., p. 5). Consequently Rousseau's education is grounded in the moral imperative to protect the natural goodness of children from the pathology of adult society. 'All of Rousseau's works concentrate on a single theme, the utopian desire to reconstruct society by means of a new theory of natural order' (Bowen, 1981, p. 188).

Beyond the Traditionalist–Progressive Divide

There can be little doubt that the ideological battle between Tate and Erricker constitutes the resurrection of a debate that has been central to the history of Western education. As such, it reinforces the polarisation of educational thinking already inherent in the tensions between Locke and Rousseau: on one side of the educational divide stand the modernists who favour a traditional subject-centred pedagogy, on the other, the romantics who advocate child-centred progressivism. The form of the debate invites us to choose between the two extremes: both camps are, in effect, battling for power in education, both seeking the right to impose their particular moral vision on children.

Activity

- Assess your reaction to the previous chapter's advocacy of education as a process of nurture.
- Are the charges of 'unwarranted conservatism' accurate?
- To what extent are progressive and traditionalist approaches to education visible in your school?
- Can you envisage ways in which traditionalism and progressivism could develop a reciprocal rather than an antagonistic relationship?

There is little value in revisiting old ground and seeking fresh insight into what is an increasingly stagnant and futile debate. Instead this chapter will proceed on the assumption that spiritual education is best served by a rapprochement that recognises the legitimate concerns of both sides of the argument. Progressivism and traditionalism are approached as complementary dimensions of a single programme of critical spiritual education. The induction of children into certain cultural norms is inevitable, and consequently we ought to accept the duty to induct children into the best tradition available, in accordance with the stated wishes of the school community as a whole. At the same time such induction must not be allowed to exclude an education concerned to cultivate in pupils the capacity for autonomous critical thinking, thereby encouraging them to assert their freedom to think for themselves, learn to make informed judgements about the cultural norms into which they are being inducted, and engage with alternative cultural possibilities.

127

Education as Negation, Deconstruction and Compensation

This section considers three overlapping attempts to establish pupil autonomy within a broadly progressive educational framework: negative education, deconstructive education and compensatory education. It is suggested that, while all three strategies have important roles to play in an education striving for pupil autonomy, taken alone they fail to overcome the problem of educational paternalism. All three, in striving to escape from the traditionalist frying pan, simply end up throwing the child into a progressive educational fire in which autonomy is nothing but a mirage.

Negative Education

As has already been noted, Rousseau advocated a form of education concerned with the nurturing of the inherent natural goodness of children rather than with the transmission of cultural norms. He thought to achieve this via a negative education marked not by any 'positive' inculcation of knowledge, but through a 'negative' attempt to protect the child from contamination by society. Such a negative education was to provide the child with: (i) unlimited scope for play; (ii) the freedom to learn in an environment devoid of external constraint; (iii) stimulus appropriate to the natural being of the individual child; and (iv) the replacement of instruction by a process of encouraging pupils to think through issues for themselves. Authentic teaching was to be concerned 'not in teaching virtue or truth, but in preserving the heart from vice and from the spirit of error' (Rousseau, 1986, p. 57).

When adopted by mainstream progressive education in the 1960s, such a negative education manifested itself in a form of child-centred education that actively avoided a subject-centred imposition of knowledge. For many such progressivism did not go far enough: alternative experimental schools battled with advocates of the deschooling of society for the progressive high ground.

All three approaches – mainstream child-centred education, alternative education and deschooling – have in common a fear that the corruption of childhood innocence by society can be caused directly by the school itself, operating as an institutional power base of society. Their programmes sought ways to protect children from the authority of formal schooling, since by limiting or undermining the institutional authority of the school one freed the child to cultivate their innate potential and natural goodness.

There are fundamental problems with this strategy:

- it is clearly impossible to completely immunise children from society, so schooling – or the absence of schooling – will inevitably transmit, whether positively or by default, a set of cultural norms and values;
- the idealistic picture of children's natural goodness and innate potential cannot simply be taken for granted;
- merely leaving children to their own devices ultimately restricts their access to those formal pedagogical processes through which they may learn appropriate ways of engaging critically with the society they are part of.

In reality, the pretence of separation from society, coupled with the demand that children rely unaided on their innate abilities, far from being a recipe for autonomy, actually constitute an uncritical induction into a romantic ideology.

Deconstructive Education

Negative education sought to protect children from being contaminated by a corrupt society. Deconstructive education, closely associated with the post-modern world-view, accepts that such protection is impossible: it is simply not possible to place children in a protective pre-social vacuum. Pupils will always be moulded by the society around them, and the rhetoric of progressive education fails to disguise the fact that children taught within a progressive environment are simply being inducted into a romantic world-view. What is needed, according to post-modern educational-ists, is not isolation from culture, but the ability to deconstruct the ideological powers embedded within culture.

Children must be brought to an awareness that the educational systems that surround them are always ideologically rooted. Even the radical option of a de-schooled society imposes a particular anti-educational world-view on children. Post-modern education is concerned to break the spell of all such ideological discourses by empowering children to deconstruct them for themselves. They are to be taught how to cultivate the art of post-modern irony through the skill of continu-ously placing their educational experiences 'under-erasure'. Pupils must become critical about the formal curriculum placed before them and learn to recognise the traces of alternative discourses and supplement 'official' texts with alternative narra-tives. They must not allow themselves to be confined to a single educational site, but instead must learn the art of surfing the educational web to encounter an unlimited range of pedagogic possibilities. Deconstructive education requires pupils to resist being constrained by the narrow curricular perspectives transmitted to them – whether they be traditionalist or progressive in form – and instead insists that they become autodidactic, capable of constructing their own post-modern realities. For Parker, a post-modern education will encourage teachers and students

> to become ironic in reconciling the foundationless status of their beliefs and commitments – and the commitments of others – with the desire to create, develop and defend them ... The effect of a deconstructive education will leave students and teachers able to exhibit the textual, political and ideological devices and perspectives inherent in all texts; able to expose the intrinsic metaphors and characters of any example of educational dialogue. They will recognise that each position, each commitment or belief is contingent: its foun-dations are epiphenomena of its narrative; its truths are symbols which conceal a politics and an ethics; its overt story hides a covert message; it is, in short, a metaphor of a way of life, a view of education.
>
> (Parker, 1997, pp. 142f.)

At the risk of stating the obvious, such a deconstructive process operates within the normative framework of post-modern philosophy, and as such imposes a post-modern world-view on the entire educational process. Here the child's only freedom is to play in the post-modern playground, since the rejection of the hermeneutic of deconstruction in favour of the alternatives of rationalism, romanticism or critical realism, is simply not on the agenda. Consequently the child is forced into a peda-gogical process in which their learning tumbles through a host of relativistic options without any order, meaning or purpose beyond that of the satisfaction of the post-modern desire to avoid boredom. As with negative education, so deconstructive education offers only a limited autonomy to pupils, and remains inextricably rooted in a distinctive ideological framework.

Compensatory Education

Compensatory education constitutes a third attempt to combat the perceived ills of the modern education system. It accepts that negative education offers an impossible ideal, and that deconstructive education simply leaves children in an anarchic vacuum. Compensatory education is more willing to identify the specific ills of society, and to propose concrete alternatives in the form of curricular programmes that offer pupils access to genuine options otherwise unavailable to them.

Examples of such compensatory education operating outside of the framework of state schooling are to be found in the supplementary classes established by minority religious groups – especially sections of the Islamic community and some of the Black-led Christian churches – as a means of compensating their children for the ongoing threat of the erosion of their fundamental beliefs and practices by the twin processes of secularism and pluralism.

In the specific field of spiritual education David Hay is perhaps the leading advo-cate of compensatory education. It has already been noted how his empirical research led him to the conclusion that modern society has instilled a widespread suspicion of spiritual experience among the population as a whole, despite its continuing prevalence on the margins of society. Such marginalisation of spiritual awareness is the result of the fact that, in our prevailing scientific culture, 'we have difficulty in hanging on to the spiritual, because "really" the fundamentals of the world are particles and space' (Hay, 1985, p. 140). Consequently Hay emphasises the need to compensate for this materialistic dumbing-down of spiritual experience through a programme of learning designed specifically to re-sensitise children's natural capacity for spiritual awareness.

Compensatory education, unlike the strategies of negative and deconstructive education, is willing to actively protect pupils from the ills of society by presenting them with specific and clearly defined alternatives. This process, however, brings us full circle: freedom from the failings of contemporary society simply becomes the imposition of alternative world-views in a paternalistic manner that does little to enhance the autonomy and freedom of pupils.

Activity

- Clarify the distinctions between 'negative', 'deconstructive' and 'compensatory' forms of progressive education.
- To what extent are these three approaches visible in your school?
- Is the suggestion that all three ultimately embody paternalistic forms of pedagogy a viable one?
- Are there ways in which all three might have a role to play in a critical pedagogy?

It would certainly be too sweeping to dismiss the projects of negative, deconstructive and compensatory education out of hand. Their significance lies in their recognition of the dangers inherent in education as nurture, and their desire to protect and enhance the freedom of children. However, in each case the search for freedom has resulted in the imposition of an alternative ideological framework:

- negative education imposes the ideology that children's natural untutored instincts are always right, and denies them access to the positive development of their critical faculties;
- deconstructive education imposes the ideology that there is no ultimate meaning and purpose in life other than that which pupils learn to create for themselves;
- compensatory education simply inducts children into an alternative ideological world-view that – whether for secular or religious reasons – has been deemed to be preferable to the status quo.

All three processes are inextricably bound up with a variety of ideological commitments and as a result fail to establish a viable foundation for a critical spiritual education.

Emancipation through Critical Empowerment

Contemporary education has failed to develop a genuinely critical edge; instead the rhetoric of freedom and emancipation, once translated into practice, offers no more than a benign form of educational paternalism. Debate surrounding the teaching of controversial issues is regularly reduced to the level of a battle for the right to impose one particular ideological perspective in the classroom. Curriculum development in controversial areas such as spirituality proceeds on the basis that 'might is right': the political victor gains the right to impose the value system they believe to be appropriate on our children's curriculum.

What is needed is not better political debate – though this would indeed be welcome – but a form of curriculum development that deliberately sets out to enable pupils to grapple with the issues for themselves. At present there is no sustained tradition of using the tensions inherent within any given controversial situation as the starting point for a critical pedagogy. True freedom demands a structural trans-formation in the educational process that seeks to achieve children's emancipation through the development of their critical awareness. A key criterion in curriculum selection needs to be that of the extent to which the material content of the curriculum establishes a diversity of contrasting viewpoints. An appropriate presen-tation of a controversial issue ought to allow pupils to gain access to a variety of options, enable them to engage critically with the issues, and equip them to take personal responsibility for the choices they make.

Paulo Freire: Education as 'Conscientisation'

The Brazilian educator Paulo Freire is perhaps the leading advocate of such a critical education (Freire, 1972). His advocacy of an emancipatory education is rooted in his concern for the poor and dispossessed: those social outcasts and cultural aliens trapped by oppressive economic, political and ideological power structures. He rejects what he terms a 'banking' model of education committed to the transmission of pre-packed nuggets of ideological truth and behavioural norms. It is important here to recognise that both traditionalist and progressive approaches to education represent types of 'banking' education: the rhetoric of 'Behave this way because this is what mainstream society expects of you', and 'Don't listen to what others teach you, have the courage to follow your own feelings and instincts', are remarkably similar in their attempts to impose intellectual and behavioural norms on children.

Freire argues that an emancipatory education needs to embrace a strategy of 'conscientisation'. This is more than mere consciousness raising. Children must be enabled, through appropriate teaching and skill formation, to break through to an awareness of the ideological structures at work in their lives as this is manifested in their schooling, their cultural and socio-economic backgrounds, their peer groups and in society at large. Freire seeks to cultivate not just awareness, but critical awareness. Pupils must be enabled to identify and articulate their own spiritual presuppositions, however complex, confused and even contradictory these may be, and to locate these in the broader map of society, history, culture and ideas. Critical awareness demands that children are enabled to steer their way responsibly and reflectively through the complex terrain of a diversity of spiritual options.

The fact that they will inevitable encounter this terrain through their normal social relationships outside of the formal educational system makes the negative attempt to isolate and protect them from it a waste of time. To encourage them merely to embrace the habit of deconstruction by treating each spiritual option they encounter as being as good as any other, simply reduces them to accepting a spiritual relativism in which ultimate value and truth is no more than personal preference. To compensate children with alternative frameworks that depart from the prevailing norm simply replaces one form of ideological transmission with another.

Instead, children must learn to recognise that they are already located within the controversial terrain of spirituality whether they like it or not, and that critical engagement with a diversity of contrasting traditions demands reflective judgement as to what constitutes the ultimate meaning, purpose and truth of their lives.

Critical Education

Critical education is not merely a theoretical construction: critical awareness, and the possibility of establishing intelligent ownership of our spiritual beliefs in the light of alternative options, opens up the possibility of both personal and political formation and change. Spiritual education cannot be reduced to the ordering and organisation of our inner space. Mere 'head knowledge' spills out into the possibility of emancipatory practice. The consequence of such emancipatory learning is the establishment of a level of personal and community empowerment that points towards to the possibility of increasing humanisation, not merely of our minds, but of our social and political structures and systems.

Critical education is rooted in the possibility of genuine educational emancipation and empowerment. Such spiritual emancipation certainly needs a measure of critical distance, but not in the form of a wholesale negative education; it requires deconstruction, but only as a path towards the achievement of critical reconstruction; it demands the compensatory introduction of alternative spiritual traditions, provided these alternatives are not enforced but rather offered up for critical consideration. Because pupils are given genuine choice between conflicting options, and because they are taught the skills, knowledge and sensibility to explore the spiritual terrain and identify their position within it, they are able to achieve genuine emancipation. This is not to suggest that critical emancipation is devoid of ideological commitments; it is, however, to suggest that ideological commitment to the principle of an informed critical reflection that results in a genuine spiritual literacy is an ideological commitment preferable to any others currently on offer.

Activity

- Brainstorm your response to the proposal of a critical spiritual education.
- What are its chief strengths and weaknesses?
- Are there crucial issues that have not been addressed?
- To what extent is it a practical option?

Spiritual Education and the Search for Truth

At the heart of critical spiritual education stands the search for ultimate meaning and truth. Consideration of this issue brings us back to Paul Hirst's proposal for an education rooted in the various 'forms of knowledge' that played an important role at the start of the spirituality debate in the 1970s. Though his attempt to transcend the polarity between traditionalism and progressivism by equating education with the search for knowledge has since been eclipsed, there is nevertheless much to be learnt from his educational philosophy.

For Hirst, 'the debates between progressives and traditionalists are largely anachronistic' (Hirst and Peters, 1970, p. 131). He rejects traditionalism on the grounds that it entails an authoritarian method of teaching 'to which the most desirable form of response on the part of the learner is the unquestioning acceptance of doctrines', and which values 'obedience more than ... independence of mind' (ibid., pp. 29, 32). Authentic knowledge cannot be reduced to a mere authoritarian transmission of facts, and authentic induction into a cultural tradition demands a genuinely rational engagement with it. 'The acquisition of knowledge is itself a development of mind ... to fail to acquire knowledge of a certain fundamental kind, is to fail to achieve rational mind in this significant respect' (ibid., p. 32). Progressive education, characterised as an education in which the cultivation of personal virtue is paramount, is for Hirst just as flawed as traditionalism. Advocates of progressivism, he argues, do not

> sufficiently appreciate that these virtues are vacuous unless people are provided with the forms of knowledge and experience to be critical, creative and autonomous with. People have to be trained to think critically; it is not some dormant seed that flowers naturally ... being critical must be distinguished from being merely contra-suggestible, just as being 'creative' must be distinguished from mere self-expression.
>
> (ibid., pp. 31f.)

Thus, for Hirst, the achievement of knowledge cannot be distinguished from the development of the self, and the development of the self is inconceivable without the achievement of knowledge. Hirst thus seeks to overcome the dichotomy between progressivism and traditionalism by advocating a liberal education rooted in the simultaneous development of character and knowledge. This is not to be mistaken for a reductive liberalism limited merely to the induction of children into the values of freedom, tolerance and wisdom, but rather constitutes a holistic liberalism in which the liberal virtues support the ongoing quest for truth.

For Hirst liberal education is rooted in knowledge itself: all false and spurious knowledge is worthless, and character formation dislocated from actual reality leads merely to false consciousness. Thus, for example, a Christian who holds fast to the core of traditional Christian dogma and attempts to live a virtuous life in accordance with the truth of Christianity is ultimately deluded if the Christian story is not indeed true.

A number of significant revisions need to be made to Hirst's basic position, though these do not affect the substance of his argument:

- the contingency of knowledge needs to be stressed, and the 'forms of knowledge' treated not as closed systems but as open-ended linguistic clusters that provide the basic tools with which to conduct the search for a realistic understanding of reality;
- the stress on rational thought needs to give way to a broader notion of human wisdom;
- the essential connection between belief and knowledge needs to be accepted, and due recognition given to the priority of informed belief over verifiable fact in our developing understanding of ourselves and our world;

- the importance of the struggle for knowledge needs to be upheld in the light of the fact that knowledge is normally contingent and rooted in provisional judgements.

Given these qualifications, Hirst's position offers a viable foundation for critical spiritual education grounded in the search for spiritual truth.

Teaching Spirituality as a Controversial Issue

What, then, of explicit spiritual teaching? If spiritual education is driven by the search for ultimate truth, then it has to be approached as a controversial subject. Despite the received wisdom that the National Curriculum is concerned with nothing more than the transmission of 'factual' knowledge and the induction of children in established norms of moral behaviour, recent QCA initiatives and guidance have been concerned to advocate a skills-based learning and stress the importance of a critical engagement with controversial issues.

QCA guidance for Citizenship Education, for example, envisages the nurturing of a critical involvement in the political process: teachers should encourage the emergence of 'an active and politically-literate citizenry convinced that they can influence government and community affairs in the world' (QCA, 1999b, p. 5). This requires 'skills of enquiry and communication, and participation and responsible action' (ibid., p. 6). Citizenship, like spirituality, is clearly approached as a controversial subject that requires a critical education, rather than a traditionalist subject demanding mere cultural inculcation.

Activity

- Critically review a lesson you have recently taught that involved an element of spiritual education.
- How might that lesson have been taught differently within the critical framework advocated in this chapter?
- How might the guidelines on teaching controversial issues shape your future approach to spiritual pedagogy?

The fact that the present advocacy of critical spiritual education is in line with current government advice suggests that it should be treated not as an idealistic proposal relevant only to some future golden age of education, but rather as an option that is both realistic and achievable. Indeed, such a critical education is required by law, since Section 407 of the 1996 Education Act requires that 'when controversial issues are brought to pupils' attention, they are offered a balanced presentation of opposing views' (QCA, 1999a, p. 26).

Government advice on teaching controversial issues needs to be applied directly to spiritual education (ibid., pp. 25–27). By freely drawing on and adapting this advice we can propose the following targets for teachers committed to critical spiritual education:

1   Engage with spirituality as a controversial issue by refusing to shelter pupils from sensitive and controversial spiritual issues.
2   Enable pupils to encounter a diverse range of spiritual traditions by doing the following:

    (i)   ensuring that they have access to balanced information and differing views on which they can then clarify their own opinions and beliefs;

    (ii)   presenting them with information in a manner open to alternative interpretation or qualification or contradiction;

    (iii)   adopting strategies that will teach them how to recognise bias, evaluate evidence put before them, look for different interpretations, views and sources of evidence, and give reasons for what they say and do.

3   Encourage the emergence of spiritual literacy by doing the following:

    (i)   promoting development in pupils of the skills of listening, accepting difference and otherness, arguing a case, dealing with conflict and distinguishing between fact and opinion;

    (ii)   welcoming genuine and open debate.

4   Show sensitivity towards pupils by doing the following:

    (i)   recognising and catering for the need of individuals;

    (ii)   applying ground rules of behaviour and establishing an appropriate classroom climate;

    (iii)   judging when pupil discussions should, or should not, be confidential.

5   Guard against the imposition of the teacher's own spiritual views by doing the following:

    (i)   resisting the inclination to highlight a particular selection of facts or items at the expense of other equally significant ones;

    (ii)   deciding how far they are prepared to express their own beliefs, recognising their authority and influence and accepting the need to work within the school's value system;

    (iii)   avoiding setting themselves up as sole authority on matters of opinion as well as fact.

Summary

- At the core of this chapter stands the suggestion that the process of education as nurture described in the previous chapter must be supplemented by a process of education as critical emancipation.
- A review of the debate between Erricker and Tate drew the suggestion progressive and traditionalist approaches to education are best seen as complementary processes.

- The presentation of three attempts to establish a foundation for critical education – negative, deconstructive and supplementary – led to the conclusion that ultimately all three do no more than advocate a benign educational paternalism.
- Paulo Freire's advocacy of an emancipatory education concerned to empower the dispossessed suggested that cultivating the skills of critical reflection within a context of cultural pluralism provides the most appropriate foundation for critical education.
- It was then suggested that any viable critical spiritual education must be concerned with the search for ultimate spiritual truth, and that as a result spirituality must always be taught as a controversial issue that demands the cultivation of appropriate levels of spiritual literacy.

13 Conclusion

Part I: The Landscape of Spirituality

We began our investigation of spirituality in education by suggesting that our spiritual lives are marked by a need to wrestle with questions of the meaning and purpose of life, of our origin and destiny, and of the ultimate nature and truth of reality. The sheer complexity of spirituality in contemporary Britain makes the need for effective spiritual education all the more urgent. However, this complexity also constitutes a significant stumbling block, since authentic spiritual education requires teachers to be personally engaged in the spiritual quest of humanity, and in possession of appropriate levels of spiritual literacy. As a result, we elected to begin by exploring the intricate landscape of contemporary spirituality and identifying some of its key contours, landmarks and features.

- We identified materialism, romanticism, post-modernism and critical realism as four important philosophical traditions and noted how each addresses the question of spirituality in different ways and with contrasting results.
- We noted that spiritual pluralism is closely linked with the fragmentation and diversification of religion, observed that the acceptance or rejection of religious belief will automatically play a significant role in shaping our spiritual lives, and identified the tensions between varieties of atheism, forms of secular and religious fundamentalism, and types of religious orthodoxy, liberalism and radicalism.
- We reviewed the psychological evidence for the persistence of significant levels of spiritual experience, and observed that such experience appears to continue to play a formative role in the development of our sense of spiritual identity despite being increasingly estranged from the practices and beliefs of formal religion.
- From the perspective of sociology we described the decline of institutional religious practice, the failure of atheism to consolidate itself in the public consciousness, and the emergence of the post-modern phenomena of 'believing without belonging', with its diverse range of eclectic privatised spiritual beliefs and practices.

Part II: Contemporary Spiritual Education

Having explored the contours of spirituality in contemporary Britain we turned to a consideration of the theory and practice of spiritual education. We reviewed the historical development of the subject, described the crucial legislation of the 1988 Education Reform Act and noted subsequent issues and trends. The unresolved tension between inclusive and exclusive approaches to spiritual pedagogy was then identified as a key issue.

- Inclusivism proceeds by constructing a 'common-denominator' model of spirituality that seeks to reflect commonly held spiritual assumptions, establish public consensus, and present a single coherent framework for spiritual education. We criticised this position, suggesting that it failed to do justice to specific spiritual traditions, was unable to establish a viable model of learning, and side-stepped the issue of spiritual truth.
- Exclusivism proceeds by attempting to establish a specific model of spirituality and thereby avoid the vacuous nature of inclusivism. We explored the Christian exclusivism of Adrian Thatcher, the theological universalism of David Hay, the secular atheism of Mike Newby and the post-modernism of Clive Erricker, and suggested that – despite their material differences – all four advocate pedagogies are at best benignly paternalistic and at worst overtly indoctrinatory.
- Recognising the need for a critical pedagogy capable of transcending the inclusive–exclusive divide, we turned for assistance to John Hull's advocacy of a liberal spirituality that promised to enable pupils to take critical responsibility for their own spirituality development. If, at the end of the day, Hull's instinct to prioritise the liberal principles of freedom and tolerance over that of reason resulted in a further example of educational paternalism, his opening up of the possibility of a critical spiritual education was seen as being of fundamental importance to the future of the subject.

Part III: Towards a Critical Spiritual Education

Finally, we attempted to develop a critical pedagogy for spiritual education. We began by establishing a number of basic principles of critical spiritual education and then proceeded to propose a new critical agenda that highlighted the importance of issues of tradition, truth and critical thinking. We then went on to suggest that effective spiritual education must balance a hermeneutic of nurture with a hermeneutic of critical thinking.

- We suggested that education as nurture represents the major tradition of Western educational thought and argued that such nurture must take account of both national values and the specific spiritual tradition of the individual school community. Grounding spiritual education in this way demands a self-conscious advocacy of the importance of each school's ethos and of Collective Worship or shared assembly.
- We then insisted that spiritual education as nurture requires supplementing with a critical spiritual education. Distinguishing critical spiritual pedagogy from negative, deconstructive and compensatory routes, we presented it in terms of a process of critical empowerment rooted in the search for truth and the recognition that spirituality is a vital yet fundamentally controversial issue.

Further Reading

Best, R. (ed.) (1996) *Education, Spirituality and the Whole Child*, London: Cassell.
An influential collection of essays covering a broad range of issues.

Coles, R. (1992) *The Spiritual Life of Children*, London: HarperCollins.
A sensitive, stimulating and illuminating cross-cultural investigation of children's spiritual experience. Essential reading.

Copley, T. (2000) *Spiritual Development in the State School: A Perspective on Worship and Spirituality in the Education System of England and Wales*, Exeter: University of Exeter Press.
A concise and accessible introductory text.

Erricker, C., Erricker, J., Ota, C., Sullivan, D. and Fletcher, M. (1997) *The Education of the Whole Child*, London: Cassell.
Research into children's spirituality conducted from a post-modern perspective.

Hay, D. with Nye, R. (1998) *The Spirit of the Child*, London: HarperCollins.
A clear account of research into children's spirituality conducted within the tradition instigated by Alistair Hardy.

Hull, J.M. (1988) *Utopian Whispers: Moral, Religious and Spiritual Values in Schools*, Norwich: Religious and Moral Education Press.
Spiritual education approached with a combination of humanitarian instinct and down-to-earth wisdom.

Parsons, G. (ed.) (1993) *The Growth of Religious Diversity: Britain from 1945*, 2 vol, London: Routledge/Open University Press.
Despite concentrating on religious issues, these volumes present a masterful survey of the current state of spirituality in Britain.

SCAA (1995) *Spiritual and Moral Development. SCAA Discussion Papers No. 3*, London: SCAA.
A key document, offering official guidance on the nature of spirituality and the task of spiritual education.

Thatcher, A. (ed.) (1999) *Spirituality and the Curriculum*, London: Cassell.
A collection of papers highlighting religious and theological issues.

Wright, A. (1998) *Spiritual Pedagogy. A Survey, Critique and Reconstruction of Contemporary Spiritual Education in England and Wales*, Abingdon: Culham College.
Report of a research project examining the theoretical basis of contemporary spiritual education.

—— (1999) *Discerning the Spirit. Teaching Spirituality in the Religious Education Classroom*, Abingdon: Culham College.
A shorter and more accessible teacher-friendly version of the previous item, drawing conclusions for classroom practice.

141

References

Archambault, R.D. (ed.) (1965) *Philosophical Analysis and Education*, London: Routledge & Kegan Paul.

Astley, J. and Francis, L.J. (1996) (eds) *Christian Theology and Religious Education: Connections and Contradictions*, London: SPCK.

Ayer, A. J. (1971) *Language, Truth and Logic*, Harmondsworth: Penguin Books.

Ball, S. (ed.) (1990) *Foucault and Education*, London: Routledge.

Barr, J. (1980) *Explorations in Theology 7: The Scope and Authority of the Bible*, London: SCM.

Bates, D. (1996) 'Christianity, Culture and Other Religions (Part 2): F.H. Hilliard, Ninian Smart and the 1988 Education Reform Act', *British Journal of Religious Education*, 18:2, pp. 85–102.

Beck, J. (1999) "Spiritual and Moral Development' and Religious Education' in A. Thatcher (ed.) *Spirituality and the Curriculum*, London: Cassell, pp. 153–180.

Beiser, F.C. (1998) 'A Romantic Education: The Concept of Bildung in Early German Romanticism' in A.O. Rorty (ed.) *Philosophers of Education: New Historical Perspectives*, London: Routledge, pp. 284–299.

Bernstein, R.J. (1983) *Beyond Objectivism and Relativism: Science, Hermeneutics and Praxis*, Oxford: Basil Blackwell.

Best, R. (ed.) (1996) *Education, Spirituality and the Whole Child*, London: Cassell.

BHA (1999) British Humanist Association Website, *http://www.humanism.org.uk/* (accessed December 1999).

Bhaskar, R. (1993) *Dialectic: The Pulse of Freedom*, London: Verso.

Bowen, J. (1981) *A History of Western Education. Volume Three: The Modern West*, London: Methuen.

Bruce, S. (1996) *Religion in the Modern World: From Cathedrals to Cults*, Oxford: Oxford University Press.

Buckley, M.J. (1987) *At the Origins of Modern Atheism*, New Haven, CT: Yale University Press.

Byrne, J. (1996) *Glory, Jest and Riddle: Religious Thought in the Enlightenment*, London: SCM.

Callaghan, J. (1976) 'Towards a National Debate', *Education*, 148:17, 132–133.

Carr, D. (1996) 'Rival Conceptions of Spiritual Education', *Journal of Philosophy of Education*, 30:2, 159–178.

—— (1998a) 'Introduction: The Post-war Rise and Fall of Educational Epistemology' in D. Carr (ed.) *Education, Knowledge and Truth. Beyond the Postmodern Impasse*, London: Routledge, pp. 1–15.

References

—— (ed.) (1998b) *Education, Knowledge and Truth. Beyond the Postmodern Impasse*, London: Routledge.

Chadwick, P. (1997) *Shifting Alliances: Church and State in English Education*, London: Cassell.

Coles, R. (1992) *The Spiritual Life of Children*, London: HarperCollins.

Collier, A. (1994) *Critical Realism. An Introduction to Roy Bhaskar's Philosophy*, London: Verso.

Connolly, P. (ed.) (1999) *Approaches to the Study of Religion*, London: Cassell.

Conrad, J. (1999) *Heart of Darkness*, Harmondsworth: Penguin Books.

Copley, T. (1997) *Teaching Religion: Fifty Years of Religious Education in England and Wales*, Exeter: University of Exeter Press.

—— (2000) *Spiritual Development in the State School: A Perspective on Worship and Spirituality in the Education System of England and Wales*, Exeter: University of Exeter Press.

Cupitt, D. (1980) *Taking Leave of God*, London: SCM.

——. (1987) *The Long-Legged Fly: A Theology of Language and Desire*, London: SCM.

Davie, G. (1994) *Religion in Britain Since 1945: Believing Without Belonging*, Oxford: Blackwell.

Derrida, J. (1976) *Of Grammatology*, Baltimore: Johns Hopkins University Press.

Derrida, J. and Vattimo, G. (eds) *Religion*, Cambridge: Polity Press.

DES (1977) *Education in Our Schools*, London: HMSO.

DES/HMI (1977a) *Curriculum 11–16*, London: HMSO.

—— (1997b) *Supplement to Curriculum 11–16*, London: HMSO.

Descartes, R. (1969) *Discourse on Method and the Meditations*, Harmondsworth: Penguin Books.

DFE (1994) *Religious Education and Collective Worship. Circular 1/94*, London: DFE.

Durkheim, E. (1971) *The Elementary Forms of the Religious Life*, London: George Allen & Unwin.

Eliade, M. (1987) *The Sacred and the Profane: The Nature of Religion*, London: Harvester/Harcourt Brace.

Eliot, T.S. (1974) 'Burnt Norton', in *Collected Poems 1909–1962*, London: Faber & Faber.

Erricker, C. (1993) 'The Iconic Quality of the Mind', in D. Starkings (ed.) *Religion and the Arts in Education: Dimensions of Spirituality*, London: Hodder & Stoughton, pp. 138–195.

Erricker, C. and Erricker, J. (1999) 'Spiritual and Moral Development: A Suitable Case for Treatment', in A. Thatcher (ed.) *Spirituality and the Curriculum*, London: Cassell, pp. 121–141.

—— (2000) 'Spirituality in the Classroom', in A. Wright and A-.M Brandon (eds) *Learning to Teach Religious Education in the Secondary School: A Companion to School Experience*, London: Routledge, pp. 183–200.

Erricker, C., Erricker, J., Ota, C., Sullivan, D. and Fletcher, M. (1997) *The Education of the Whole Child*, London: Cassell.

Feuerbach, L. (1989) *The Essence of Christianity*, New York: Prometheus Books.

Fleischner, E. (ed.) (1977) *Auschwitz: Beginning of a New Era*, New York: KTAV.

Flood, G. (1999) *Beyond Phenomenology: Rethinking the Study of Religion*, London: Cassell.

Foucault, M. (1989) *The Order of Things: An Archaeology of the Human Sciences*, London: Tavistock/Routledge.

—— (1991) *The Archaeology of Knowledge*, London: Routledge.

Francis, L.J., Kay, W.K. and CampbelL, W.S. (eds) (1996) *Research in Religious Education*, Leominster: Gracewing.

Freire, P. (1972) *Pedagogy of the Oppressed*, Harmondsworth: Penguin Books.

Gadamer, H.-G. (1979) *Truth and Method*, London: Sheed and Ward.

Gay, P. (1973) *The Enlightenment: An Interpretation. Part Two: The Science of Freedom*, London: Wildwood House.

Gellner, E. (1974) *Legitimation of Belief*, Cambridge: Cambridge University Press.

Gelwick, R. (1977) *The Way of Discovery: An Introduction to the Thought of Michael Polanyi*, Oxford: Oxford University Press.

Gill, R. (1993) *The Myth of the Empty Church*, London: SPCK.

Gold, A. and Evans, J. (1998) *Reflecting on School Management*, London: Falmer.

Goldman, R. (1964) *Religious Thinking from Childhood to Adolescence*, London: Routledge & Kegan Paul.

Greenberg, I. (1977) 'Cloud of Smoke, Pillar of Fire: Judaism, Christianity, and Modernity after the Holocaust', in E. Fleischner (ed.) *Auschwitz: Beginning of a New Era*, New York: KTAV, pp. 7–55.

Grimmitt, M. (1987) *Religious Education and Human Development: The Relationship Between Studying Religions and Personal, Social and Moral Education*, Great Wakering, Essex: McCrimmon.

Gunton, C.E. (1983) *Yesterday and Today: A Study in Continuities in Christology*, London: Darton, Longman & Todd.

—— (1985) *Enlightenment and Alienation. An Essay Towards a Trinitarian Theology*, Basingstoke: Marshall, Morgan and Scott.

Halstead, J.M. (1995) 'Liberal Values and Liberal Education', in J.M. Halstead and M.J. Taylor (eds) *Values in Education and Education in Values*, London: Falmer Press, pp. 17–32.

Halstead, J.M. and Taylor, M.J. (eds) (1995) *Values in Education and Education in Values*, London: Falmer Press.

Hardy, A. (1966)*The Divine Flame*, Oxford: Manchester College.

—— (1979)*The Spiritual Nature of Man*, Oxford: Clarendon Press.

Harvey, D. (1990) *The Condition of Postmodernity; An Enquiry into the Origins of Cultural Change*, Oxford: Blackwell.

Hay, D. (1982) 'Teaching the Science of the Spirit', in J.G. Priestley (ed.) *Religion, Spirituality and Schools (Perspectives 9)*, Exeter: University of Exeter Press, pp. 37–53.

——. (1985) 'Suspicion of the Spiritual: Teaching Religion in a World of Secular Experience', *British Journal of Religious Education*, 7:3, 140–147.

Hay, D. with Nye, R. (1998) *The Spirit of the Child*, London: HarperCollins.

Hay, D., Nye, R. and Murphy, R. (1996) 'Thinking About Childhood Spirituality: Review of Research and Current Directions', in L.J. Francis, W.S. Kay and W.S. Campbell (eds) *Research in Religious Education*, Leominster: Gracewing, pp. 47–71.

Haydon, G. (1997) *Teaching About Values: A New Approach*, London: Cassell.

Heelas, P. (1996) *The New Age Movement*, Oxford: Blackwell.

Hick, J. (1977) *God and the Universe of Faiths*, London: Collins.

Hill, B.V. (1989) ' "Spiritual Development" in the Education Reform Act: A Source of Acrimony, Apathy or Accord?', *British Journal of Educational Studies*, 37:2, 169–182.

Hirst, P.H. (1965) 'Liberal Education and the Nature of Knowledge', in R.D. Archambault (ed.) *Philosophical Analysis and Education*, London: Routledge & Kegan Paul, pp. 113–138.

Hirst, P.H. and Peters, R.S. (1970) *The Logic of Education*, London: Routledge & Kegan Paul.

HMSO (1944) *Education Act*, London: HMSO.

—— (1985) *Education for All: The Report of the Committee of Inquiry into the Education of Children from Ethnic Minority Groups (The Swann Report)*, London: HMSO.

—— (1988) *Education Reform Act*, London: HMSO.

References

Hobson, P.R. and Edwards, J.S. (1999) *Religious Education in a Pluralist Society: The Key Philosophical Issues*, London: Woburn Press.

Holley, R. (1978) *Religious Education and Religious Understanding. An Introduction to the Philosophy of Religious Education*, London: Routledge & Kegan Paul.

Homer (1946) *The Odyssey*, Harmondsworth: Penguin Books.

Hull, J.M. (ed.) (1982) *New Directions in Religious Education*, Basingstoke: Falmer Press.

—— (1998) *Utopian Whispers: Moral, Religious and Spiritual Values in Schools*, Norwich: Religious and Moral Education Press.

Hume, D. (1978) *A Treatise of Human Nature*, Oxford: Oxford University Press.

James, W. (1960) *The Varieties of Religious Experience; A Study in Human Nature*, London: Collins.

Kay, W.K. and Francis, L.J. (1996) *Drift from the Churches: Attitude Toward Christianity During Childhood and Adolescence*, Cardiff: University of Wales Press.

King, U. (1985) 'Spirituality in Secular Society: Recovering a Lost Dimension', *British Journal of Religious Education*, 7:3, 135–139, 111.

Kuhn, T.S. (1970) *The Structure of Scientific Revolutions*, Chicago: University of Chicago Press.

Kung, H. (1980) *Does God Exist? An Answer for Today*, London: Collins.

Lash, N. (1988) *Easter in Ordinary. Reflections on Human Experience and the Knowledge of God*, London: SCM.

Lealman, B. (1982) 'The Ignorant Eye: Perception and Religious Education', *British Journal of Religious Education*, 4:2, 59–63.

—— (1986) 'Grottoes, Ghettos and City of Glass: Conversations about Spirituality', *British Journal of Religious Education*, 8:2, 65–71.

Levin, D.M. (1988) *The Opening of Vision. Nihilism and the Postmodern Situation*, London: Routledge.

Lindbeck, G.A. (1984) *The Nature of Doctrine: Religion and Theology in a Postliberal Age*, London: SPCK.

Locke, J. (1968) *The Educational Writings of John Locke*, Cambridge: Cambridge University Press.

—— (1975) *An Essay Concerning Human Understanding*, Oxford: Clarendon Press.

Lonergan, B. (1973) *Method in Theology*, London: Darton, Longman & Todd.

Lyotard, J.-F. (1984) *The Postmodern Condition: A Report on Knowledge*, Manchester: Manchester University Press.

Macquarrie, J. (1971) *Twentieth-Century Religious Thought: The Frontiers of Philosophy and Theology, 1900–1970*, London: SCM.

Maxwell, N. (1987) *From Knowledge to Wisdom: A Revolution in the Aims and Methods of Science*, Oxford: Blackwell.

Newbigin, L. (1982) 'Teaching Religion in a Secular Plural Society', in J. Hull (ed.) *New Directions in Religious Education*, Basingstoke: Falmer Press, pp. 97–107.

Newby. M. (1994) 'The Spiritual Development of Children in a Secular Context: Reflections on some Aspects of Theory and Practice', *SPES*, 1, 17–20.

—— (1996) 'Towards a Secular Concept of Spiritual Maturity,' in R. Best (ed.) *Education, Spirituality and the Whole Child*, London: Cassell, pp. 93–107.

NCC (1993) *Spiritual and Moral Development*, York: NCC.

Norris, C. (1987) *Derrida*, London: Collins.

Northcott, M.S. (1999) 'Sociological Approaches', in P. Connolly (ed.) *Approaches to the Study of Religion*, London: Cassell, pp. 193–225.

NSC (2000) National Secular Society Website, *http://www.secularism.org.uk/* (accessed February 2000).

Outram, D. (1995) *The Enlightenment*, Cambridge: Cambridge University Press.

Parker, S. (1997) *Reflective Teaching in the Postmodern World: A Manifesto for Education in Postmodernity*, Buckingham: Open University Press.

Parsons, G. (ed.) (1993) *The Growth of Religious Diversity: Britain from 1945*, 2 vols, London: Routledge/Open University Press.

Pascal, B. (1966) *Pensées*, Harmondsworth: Penguin Books.

Plato (1963) *The Collected Dialogues*, Princeton, NJ: Princeton University Press.

Polanyi, M. (1958) *Personal Knowledge: Towards a Post-Critical Philosophy*, London: Routledge & Kegan Paul.

Popper, K.R. (1966) *The Open Society and its Enemies. Volume One: Plato*, London: Routledge & Kegan Paul.

Priestley, J.G. (1982) (ed.) *Religion, Spirituality and Schools (Perspectives 9)*, Exeter: University of Exeter Press.

—— (1985) 'Towards Finding the Hidden Curriculum: A Consideration of the Spiritual Dimension of Experience in Curriculum Planning', *British Journal of Religious Education*, 7:3, 112–119.

—— (1992) 'Whitehead Revisited – Religion and Education: An Organic Whole', in B. Watson (ed.) *Priorities in Religious Education. A Model for the 1990's and Beyond*, London: Falmer Press, pp. 26–37.

QCA (1999a) *Consultation Draft: Personal, Social and Health Education and Citizenship at Key Stages 1 and 2. Initial Guidance for Schools*, London: Qualifications and Curriculum Authority.

—— (1999b) *Citizenship at Key Stages 3 and 4. Initial Guidance for Schools*, London: Qualifications and Curriculum Authority.

Ramsey, A.E. (1999) 'Poor in Spirit? The Child's World, the Curriculum and 'Spirituality'", in A. Thatcher (ed.) *Spirituality and the Curriculum*, London: Cassell, pp. 111–123.

Reeve, C.D.C. (1998) 'Aristotelian Education', in A.O. Rorty (ed.) *Philosophers of Education: New Historical Perspectives*, London: Routledge, pp. 51–65.

Ricoeur, P. (1974) *The Conflict of Interpretations*, Evanston, ILL: Northwestern University Press.

—— (1995) *Figuring the Sacred. Religion, Narrative and Imagination*, Minneapolis: Fortress Press.

Robinson, E. (1977) *The Original Vision. A Study of the Religious Experience of Childhood*, Oxford: The Religious Experience Research Unit, Manchester College.

Rorty, A.O. (ed.) (1998) *Philosophers of Education: New Historical Perspectives*, London: Routledge.

Rorty, R. (1989) *Contingency, Irony and Solidarity*, Cambridge: Cambridge University Press.

Rousseau, J.-J. (1986) *Emile*, London: Dent.

Said, E. (1978) *Orientalism*, New York: Pantheon.

Saliba, J.A. (1995) *Perspectives on New Religious Movements*, London: Geoffrey Chapman.

SCAA (1995) *Spiritual and Moral Development. SCAA Discussion Papers No. 3*, London: SCAA.

Schleiermacher, F.D.E. (1976) *The Christian Faith*, Edinburgh: T. & T. Clark.

Sharpe, E.J. (1986) *Comparative Religion: A History*, London: Duckworth.

Slee, N. (1992) "Heaven in Ordinarie": The Imagination, Spirituality and the Arts in Religious Education', in B. Watson (ed.) *Priorities in Religious Education: A Model for the 1990's and Beyond*, London: Falmer Press, pp. 38–57.

Smith, R. and Standish, P. (eds) (1977) *Teaching Right and Wrong: Moral Education in the Balance*, Stoke on Trent, Staffordshire: Trentham Books.

References

Starkings, D. (ed.) (1993) *Religion and the Arts in Education: Dimensions of Spirituality*, London: Hodder & Stoughton.

Talbot, M. and Tate, N. (1997) 'Shared Values in a Pluralist Society', in R. Smith. and P. Standish (eds) *Teaching Right and Wrong: Moral Education in the Balance*, Stoke on Trent, Staffordshire: Trentham Books, pp. 1–14.

Tate, N. (1996) 'Education for Adult Life: Spiritual and Moral Aspects of the Curriculum', paper delivered at the SCAA Conference on Education for Adult Life, 15 January 1996, London: School Curriculum and Assessment Authority.

Taylor, C. (1992) *Sources of the Self: The Making of the Modern Identity*, Cambridge: Cambridge University Press.

Thatcher, A. (1996) ' "Policing the Sublime": A Wholly (Holy?) Ironic Approach to the Spiritual Development of Children', in J. Astley and L.J. Francis (eds) *Christian Theology and Religious Education: Connections and Contradictions*, London: SPCK, pp. 117–139.

—— (1999a) 'Theology, Spirituality and the Curriculum – An Overview', in A. Thatcher (ed.) *Spirituality and the Curriculum*, London: Cassell, pp. 1–11.

—— (1999b) 'Values – Secular or Christian?: A Response to Mary Grey', in A. Thatcher (ed.) *Spirituality and the Curriculum*, London: Cassell, pp. 33–54.

—— (ed.) (1999c) *Spirituality and the Curriculum*, London: Cassell.

Tillich, P. (1962) *The Courage to Be*, London: Collins.

—— (1978) *Systematic Theology*, vol. 1, London: SCM.

Torrance, T.F. (1980) *The Ground and Grammar of Theology*, Belfast: Christian Journals.

Vattimo, G. (1998) 'The Trace of the Trace', in J. Derrida and G. Vattimo (eds) *Religion*, Cambridge: Polity Press, pp. 79–94.

Watson, B. (1992) (ed.) *Priorities in Religious Education: A Model for the 1990's and Beyond*, London: Falmer Press.

Webster, D.H. (1982) 'Spiritual Growth in Religious Education', in D.H. Webster and M.F. Tickner (eds) *Religious Education and the Imagination. Aspects of Education: 28*, Hull: University of Hull Institute of Education, pp. 85–95.

Webster, D.H., and Tickner. M.F. (eds) (1982) *Religious Education and the Imagination. Aspects of Education: 28*, Hull: University of Hull Institute of Education.

Wittgenstein, L. (1968) *Philosophical Investigations*, Oxford: Basil Blackwell.

Wollaston, I. (1992) 'What Can – and Cannot – Be Said: Religious Language after the Holocaust', *Journal of Literature and Theology*, 6:1, 47–56.

Wolterstorff, N. (1996) *John Locke and the Ethics of Belief*, Cambridge: Cambridge University Press.

Woods, T. (1999) *Beginning Postmodernism*, Manchester: Manchester University Press.

Wright, A. (1996) 'The Child in Relationship: Towards a Communal Model of Spirituality', in R. Best (ed.) *Education, Spirituality and the Whole Child*, London: Cassell, pp. 139–149.

—— (1998) *Spiritual Pedagogy. A Survey, Critique and Reconstruction of Contemporary Spiritual Education in England and Wales*, Abingdon: Culham College.

—— (1999) *Discerning the Spirit. Teaching Spirituality in the Religious Education Classroom*, Abingdon: Culham College.

Wright, A. and Brandon, A.-M. (eds) (2000) *Learning to Teach Religious Education in the Secondary School. A Companion to School Experience*, London: Routledge.

Wu, D. (ed.) (1997) *A Companion to Romanticism*, Oxford: Blackwell Publishers.

Index